# BULGARIA

BY

LINDSAY AND PETE BENN

D1114159

Produced by
Thomas Cook Publishing

**Written by** Lindsay Bennett
**Original photography by** Pete Bennett

Edited and designed by Laburnum Technologies Pvt Ltd,
C-533 Triveni Apts, Sheikh Sarai Phase 1,
New Delhi 110017

Published by Thomas Cook Publishing
A division of Thomas Cook Tour Operations Limited

PO Box 227, Unit 15/16, Coningsby Road,
Peterborough PE3 8SB, United Kingdom
E-mail: books@thomascook.com
www.thomascookpublishing.com

ISBN: 1-841574-34-1

Head of Thomas Cook Publishing: Chris Young
Project Editor: Charlotte Christensen
Project Administrator: Michelle Warrington
DTP: Steven Collins

Series Manager: Stephen York

Printed and bound in Spain by: Grafo Industrias Graficas, Basauri

Cover design by: Liz Lyons Design, Oxford
Front cover credits: Left © Nicholas Pitt/Getty Images;
centre © Tom Tracy Photography/Alamy; right © Thomas Cook
Tour Operations Ltd.
Back cover credits: Left © Blueberg/Alamy; right © StockShot/Alamy.

| | |
|---|---|
| **c. 475** | Slavs from the Carpathian Mountains settle in the region to farm. |
| **c. 550** | Warlike Bulgars arrive from the east. |
| **681** | The First Bulgarian Empire is proclaimed by Khan (or Tsar) Asparukh. |
| **681–1018** | Slavs, Bulgars and Thracians develop a peaceful understanding as the empire expands. Tension with the Christian Byzantines is constant and fighting breaks out sporadically. |
| **c. 860** | Tsar Boris I converts Bulgarians to Christianity. |
| **893–927** | The Empire is at its height under Tsar Simeon, with a capital at Veliki Preslav, but his attempt to capture the Byzantine throne backfires. |
| **1018** | The first Bulgarian Empire comes to an end as the people are assimilated into the Byzantine Empire. |
| **1185** | Uprising leads to the Second Bulgarian Empire (including parts of modern Serbia and Hungary) with a powerful capital at Veliko Turnovo. |
| **1396** | Ottoman Turks invade Bulgaria, bringing to an end the Second Empire. |
| **1400s–1800s** | Ottoman rule. Christianity is persecuted but religious fervour is kept alive in the remote monasteries. Some Slavs convert to Islam, becoming 'Pomaks'. |
| **1762** | Monk Paisii Hilendarski completes the first comprehensive history of the Slav-Bulgarian people, kick-starting the Bulgarian National Revival. |
| **1870** | Ottoman Turks recognise the Bulgarian Orthodox Church. |
| **1876** | April Uprising against Ottoman rule is brutally put down. |
| **1877** | Russia declares war on the Ottoman Empire in defence of the Bulgarian people. Estimates put the death toll at 200,000. |
| **1878** | Treaty of San Stefano ends the Russian-Turkish War with vast tracts of the Balkan peninsula now independent Bulgarian soil. |

Monument in Vratsa to freedom fighter and national hero Hristo Botev

| | |
|---|---|
| 1878 | The Treaty of Berlin rewrites the map as Western Europe fears too much Russian influence in the region. A smaller Bulgaria becomes an independent state but this treaty creates artificial boundaries that still haunt the Balkans today. |
| 1879 | Bulgarian constitution adopted. |
| 1885 | Border problems cause short-lived war with Serbia. Western Europe recognises an expanded Bulgaria. |
| 1912 | First Balkan War against the Ottomans. Bulgaria, Serbia, Greece and Montenegro conquer Macedonia and parts of Thrace. |
| 1913 | Second Balkan War, against Serbia, Romania and Greece breaks out over sovereignty of other lands released by the Ottomans. |
| 1915 | Bulgaria enters First World War on the German side. |
| 1939 | Bulgaria declares its neutrality at the start of the Second World War. |
| 1941 | Bulgarian authorities allow German troops to enter the country. They declare war on Britain and France but not on Soviet Russia. |
| 1943 | King Boris III dies in mysterious circumstances soon after a tense meeting with Hitler. |
| 1946 | The People's Republic of Bulgaria is proclaimed with a constitution based on Soviet Russia's communist system. |

| | |
|---|---|
| **1946–1962** | The country is led by Georgi Dimitrov. |
| **1962–1989** | Todor Zhivkov takes control and Bulgaria becomes one of the most successful economies in the Eastern Bloc. |
| **1985–1989** | Perestroika weakens the foundations of the communist system across Eastern Europe. |
| **Nov 1989** | An internal coup within the Communist Party brings an end to Zhivkov's rule. The Communist Party opens up the Bulgarian political arena and changes its name to the Bulgarian Socialist Party. A group of other parties come together under the banner Union of Democratic Forces (UDF). |
| **1990** | The Bulgarian Socialist Party sweeps to victory in the first national elections since the fall of communism. |
| **1990–1997** | Seven ineffectual governments in seven years cause the collapse of the Bulgarian economy. Bribery, organised crime and corruption are rife. |

| | |
|---|---|
| **2001** | The exiled former Bulgarian King Simeon II forms a political party, the National Movement. Simeon wins the June elections, becoming prime minister, while ex-communist Parnavov becomes president. |
| **2001–2004** | The country starts on the long road to EU economic compliance and membership (now due in 2007). |
| **Mar 2004** | Bulgaria becomes a member of NATO, breaking irrevocably with its Eastern Bloc past. |

Memorial to the Martyrs of Communist Terror, Sofia

# Orthodoxy and the Monasteries

sounds of Slav. By the year 900 this had developed into the standard Cyrillic script still in use today.

The development of the written language took place during the era of Bulgaria's First Empire. Its capital Veliki Preslav was the most powerful in the Balkans. The fact that the Bulgarians could worship in their own language was immensely important. The seeds of a new Bulgarian national identity planted by Boris and successive Bulgarian Tsars thrived through use of this new language, and were nurtured by Bulgarian Orthodoxy.

The founding of religious communities became a fashionable practice; Bulgaria's leading religious community, Rila, was established at this time around the charismatic hermit/monk Ivan Rilski. The royal family and upper echelons of the court made major bequests to the most influential religious orders. The huge influxes of cash, precious gifts and relics allowed monasteries to employ the finest masons, woodcarvers and artists for the building and

Monasteries have played a pivotal role in the development of Bulgarian society and culture in the centuries since Tsar Boris converted the population to Christianity c. 860 AD.

In the early 860s, two brothers Kiril (Cyril) and Metodii (Methodius) (*see box*) were invited by the Pope to carry the words of the Gospel to the Slav people in their own language rather than in Latin. This involved translating the Bible into Slavic, a tongue for which there was no written language. The brothers set about devising an alphabet (originally called Glagolitic) incorporating all the

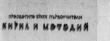

Facing page: Dryanovo Monastery
This page above: Orthodox monk; left: Sofia's statue of Sts Cyril and Methodius

decoration of their complexes, giving rise to a golden age of religious art and handicrafts.

In their turn, the monasteries repaid this patronage with their steadfastness throughout the years of Ottoman rule. They protected the faith and became the repository of Bulgarian culture in the written word, and traditional religious art in the face of a religion that was implacably opposed to iconic images as a basis for worship. Furthermore, as the yoke of Ottoman power grew heavier over time, they provided help on a practical level, offering succour and sanctuary to the freedom fighters who sought to rid the country of foreign influence.

Orthodoxy rose like a phoenix from the flames in the wake of the Ottoman

withdrawal from the Balkans in the late 19th century. Today it is emerging from behind the shadow of communism into a 21st-century Bulgaria driven by a market economy. It remains to be seen whether the monasteries will survive as thriving religious communities or simply end up as the country's primary tourist attractions.

## CYRIL AND METHODIUS

Brothers Cyril (c. 827–869) and Methodius (c. 815–895) were born in Thessalonika (now in Greece) where their father was serving in the Byzantine army.

They didn't enter the priesthood immediately. Methodius followed his father into the military before becoming a monk while Cyril (christened Constantine) chose teaching and philosophy, being at one time the chief archivist at the library in Byzantium.

The brothers travelled together throughout the Balkans, evangelising. After Cyril's untimely death, Methodius became papal delegate to the Slavic region.

In the following centuries many universities and libraries in the Balkans were named after the brothers, who were pronounced 'protectors of Europe' in 1995 by Pope John Paul II.

Website *www.bulgarianmonastery.com* offers more background info on each of the monasteries featured in the What to See section and less significant monasteries out of the scope of this guide.

# Governance

## Post-communist Bulgaria

How has Bulgaria fared since the fall of communism in 1989 and the creation of the parliamentary democracy in 1991?

Well, it didn't make a brilliant start. There were eight governments between 1991 and 1999, none with a grasp of the complexity of the job in hand. The change to a market economy caused economic meltdown, not helped by rampant corruption and the proliferation of a Bulgarian 'mafia' – a phalanx of ex-secret service officers and party officials – who were making good profits on protection rackets and money laundering.

In 1999 a new left-wing coalition with reasonably firm foundations set about introducing a series of programmes under the collective banner 'Bulgaria 2000' – designed to prepare the country for the new millennium. The plans included the revision and decentralisation of many government functions based on EU-approved models.

Then in 2001 came the surprising, almost fairytale development that holds the promise of a sustained new beginning. Ex-King Simeon declared that he was returning to the country permanently

Parliament Building, Sofia

## EX-KING SIMEON

Born in Sofia in 1937, the young Prince Simeon of Saxe-Coburg-Gotha went into exile during the Second World War. He inherited his title at the age of 6 following the untimely and mysterious death of his father Boris III in 1943.

Immediately after the war the family returned to Bulgaria but in a referendum the population rejected the constitutional monarchy and Spain offered the young King asylum.

Simeon received his education in Alexandria, Madrid and military college in the United States, following which he became a successful businessman and worked tirelessly on behalf of Bulgarian exiles with many national and international bodies. After the fall of communism he first visited Bulgaria in 1996, a full 50 years after his discomfiting departure.

and furthermore he was going to found a political party and run for elected office.

Though public demand for a constitutional monarchy was weak (only 15 per cent of those questioned felt it appropriate), the ex-monarch was still a very popular figure. Founded only two months before the elections, the new National Movement Simeon II Party took first place and Simeon was inaugurated as the new prime minister, the first European monarch ever to have gained civil power following the loss of the throne.

By 2002 the Bulgarian economy was slowly and painfully turning the corner. The monetary unit, the lev, was linked to the euro and inflation was stable at a moderate 3.8 per cent. The country began to look outward from its domestic crises and forge a coherent foreign policy. It ameliorated the crisis in Kosovo by allowing ground support forces of the UN to land and coordinate their peacekeeping strategy, and it finally broke completely with the old Soviet bloc by joining NATO in March 2004.

Its sights are now firmly set on closer ties with Europe. An accord signed in February 2004 means that Bulgaria, all convergence criteria being met, will now join the EU in 2007. Already, the majority of its international investment comes from European countries, and the majority of its exports find markets in European countries. With a current average income of only 270 leva (around £90) per month, Bulgarians are hoping they will soon see tangible financial benefits to match their new constitutional freedoms.

## The Constitution

The Bulgarian constitution upholds the National Assembly as the sole legislative body. It comprises 240 members elected every four years by proportional representation. The National Assembly then elects the prime minister.

The president is the head of state. Elected every five years, the president can service a maximum of two terms in office.

A council of 12 judges ultimately protects the constitution and the rights of citizens. They are subject to elections every nine years.

### The Bulgarian Flag
The post-communist Bulgarian flag is composed of three horizontal bands – white, green and red. White represents the land, green represents the natural riches of the countryside and red represents the courage and resilience of the people.

# Culture

Bulgarian culture is inextricably linked with its battle for national self-determination. The nation's self-image has been forged from its long and titanic struggles against the Byzantines during the First Bulgarian Empire, the Ottomans during the Second Bulgarian Empire and communism during the latter part of the 20th century.

Typical church architecture

The Bulgarian National Revival period in the late 19th century (*see pp26–7*) was the joyous expression of a people free from a heavy yoke. In present day Bulgaria it is difficult to overestimate its importance in representing all that is good in the arts.

### The Role of the Church

Perhaps more than in any other country in the world, the Church features as an important national presence, working for cultural, not just physical and spiritual, survival. In addition to nurturing Bulgarian arts and crafts, the Bulgarian Orthodox Church also acted as the custodian for important, rare and sometimes illegally produced books, allowing a newly liberated Bulgaria to re-engage with its past in the wake of the Ottoman withdrawal.

### The Freedom Fighters

The fight for freedom from the Ottoman Empire was never a peasant-led move-ment. The revolutionary committees comprised intellectuals, poets, writers and scholars, and they galvanised the common people with their call to arms. Chief amongst these was the poet Ivan Vazov (1850–1921). His works included titles such as *Deliverance, Epic of the Forgotten,* and the novel *Under the Yoke* (1894), describing life in a Bulgarian village under Ottoman rule that epitomised the struggle of the whole population. Poet Hristo Danov (depicted on today's 50 leva bank note) became one of the first post-independence publishers, helping to bring Cyrillic texts to the general population. Georgi Danchov, a classicist, is the most renowned artist of the period between independence and the Second World War.

### The Growth of the Arts in the Post-Ottoman Period

Several opera houses and theatres were built in the late 19th and early 20th century to cater to rising demand for performances. The National Academy of Arts was also formed in 1896 to formalise the burgeoning genres. However, most artistic development took place within the metaphysical boundaries of the national experience of Ottoman oppression. Expression in literature and music was often introspective rather than expansive, focusing attention inwards to Bulgarian tradition rather than exploring influences from the greater world.

Dobri Hristov (1875-1941), the most distinguished Bulgarian composer of the 20th century, is considered the father of modern Bulgarian classical music. Born in Varna, he graduated from the Prague Conservatory in 1903, following which he collaborated closely with Antonin Dvořak. Hristov inextricably linked Bulgarian classical music with the lilt, structure and cadence of traditional folk tunes. Another luminary, Emanuil Manolov (1860–1920), composed the first Bulgarian opera, *Siromahkinia*. However, Pancho Vladigerov composed in a more mainstream western tradition and is perhaps the best-known composer of the period outside Bulgaria.

In the literary world, Greek-born Atanas Dalchev (1904–1978) wrote well-received novels during the 20s and 30s and poetess/writer Elisaveta Bagriyana (1893–1991) also published her best works at this time. She was one of the first authors to be studied in school and university literature classes and still features in current syllabuses.

Painting was evolving too – moving from the classic to more experimental styles taking into account the arrival of Impressionism and Surrealism in Europe. Anton Mitov, son of a master icon painter, was at the forefront of the movement, along with Jaroslav Preshin.

Dobrich Ethnological Museum showcases traditional Bulgarian craftwork

Ruse Theatre

## The Arts under Communism

Even before the end of the Second World War, the steely reach of the Soviet regime cast a dark shadow over the arts. Rayko Alexiev (1893–1944), a renowned cartoonist and writer, was beaten to death by unknown culprits after publishing several anti-Soviet cartoons. This set the scene for communist rule. All forms of 'western style' composition in words and music were classed as subversive. Artists had to toe the line or fall from favour, or worse.

However, folk music was considered close to the socialist ideal and was encouraged, which strengthened the Balkan classical genre, cadences of folk music introduced by Dobri Hristov (*see previous page*). Lubumir Pipkov was a successful proponent of the approved 'socialist realism' musical style and Philip Kutev, famed for his ability to adapt folk music for the grander stage, received particular acclaim. Only later in the era, during the 1970s and 80s, did young composers such as Tsenko Minkin and Stefan Dragostinov begin to push the boundaries, experimenting with new musical forms.

During communist rule, members of the Writers Union were paid for each work they produced as long as it fitted the strict pro-Soviet criteria, no matter what the sales. This, and having to work within the constraints of the system, stilted creativity. Criticism in any form, even through the arts, was punished. Poetess Blaga Dimitrova (1922–2003) was at first feted by the communist authorities then vilified and dropped from the inner circle and Antenas Dalchev chose to remain creatively silent throughout the Zhivkov era.

The best-known Bulgarians went into exile rather than work under the Soviet yoke. The most famous of these is perhaps Georgi Markov (1929–1978). The dissident writer was working as a broadcaster for the BBC World service in London when he was struck with an umbrella tip while waiting at a bus stop. The tip deposited a small pellet containing a lethal dose of the poison ricin into his leg. He died three days later.

Others include artist Christo (Javecheff), born in 1935 in Gabrovo, renowned for his 'packaging' art – large-scale projects including the packaging of 11 islands in Biscayne Bay in Miami with pink polystyrene fabric walls – and

Stephen Grouev (born 1922), a Bulgarian political immigrant who is most famed for his book *Crown of Thorns*.

Still, the communist regime's patronage of the arts was generous. Funding of companies and training for the gifted was as important as their better-known sports programmes, which produced a generation of sporting superstars. Opera was a particular success, with Nickolai Guaurov and soprano Raina Kabaivanska making their presence felt in a competitive genre, as well as Boris Christov (born 1924), considered one of the greatest basses in opera history.

## The Arts in Post-communist Bulgaria

Since the fall of communism, intellectuals and artists have suffered a considerable downturn in fortune. State funding is almost non-existent and when the economy plunged into freefall in the 1990s it left the population no money for the 'higher' pursuits. There was an exodus from Bulgaria and many artists left for Europe and the United States, including critic Alexander Kyosev and writer Ivalyo Divchev.

Young composers such as Angel Stankov and Josif Radinov have won domestic and international acclaim for their work. The most successful writer in Bulgaria during the early 1990s was Christo Kalchev, with his title *The Wrestlers* – an exposé of the Bulgarian mafia – while writers Zlatomir Zlatanov and Roumen Leonidov, novelists Deyan Enev and Alek Popov, and poet Kristin Dimitrova all carry the torch forward into the third millennium.

The major enduring problem for writers and poets continues to be reaching a wider market and having the opportunity to be published in a language other than Bulgarian. It's also a problem that continues to hinder an outsider's enjoyment of the work of these influential thinkers.

### Across the Galaxy

A traditional Bulgarian folklore tune, 'Izlel e Deliu Haidutin' from the Rodopi region, was one of only 10 songs chosen to be included in a CD representative of 'Earth music' that was part of the cargo on the Voyager spacecraft launched in the 1970s to communicate with any other life forms in our solar system. The 10 were chosen to express as fully as possible traditional musical forms from across the planet.

Varna Opera House

# Festivals and Events

The range of festivals and events in Bulgaria is wide, reflecting the diverse lifestyles of the country. World-acclaimed celebrations of performing arts sit side by side with age-old festivities – including traditional costumes, local dances and reverential religious processions. Every crop has its own 'harvest festival', from the grape to the grain.

Traditional costume at a folk festival

The following is a list of the major festivals and events that take place each year around the country but for further details on arts festivals, *see p153.*

## March
**Varna Song Competition**
**Music Days Festival,** Ruse (last two days of the month)
**Sandanski Celebrations** (Thursday after Orthodox Easter)
**Annunciation Day,** nationwide celebrations (25th)

## April
**First Folkloric Festival,** Melnik
**Music Festival,** Shiroka Lûka (mid-month for one week)

## May
**Celebration of the April Uprising,** including re-enactment of the battle, Koprivshtitsa (1st and 2nd).
**St Kiril and St Metodii Day,** nationwide celebrations (11th)
**Balkan Folk Festival,** Veliko Turnovo (10 days in the early part of the month)
**International Plovdiv Fair** (one week mid-month)
**Days of Shumen Cultural Festival** (mid-month)

**Festival of Bansko Traditions** (one week mid-month)
**Varna Summer Festival** – the highlight of the summer along the Black Sea Coast, lasting from May to October.

## June
**Children's Day** – nationwide celebrations (1st)
**Fire Dancing Festival,** Bulgari, Strandjha Nature Park (early in the month)
**Festival of the Roses,** Kazanluk and Karlovo (early in the month)
**International Festival of Chamber Music,** Plovdiv (10 days mid-month)
**Madara Music Days Festival** (one month mid-Jun–mid-July)
**International Folklore Festival,** Veliko Turnovo (3 weeks late June–mid-July)
**Cultural Month,** Plovdiv (throughout the month, spilling over into July)

## July
**Burgas Sea Song Festival** (2 months through July–August)

## August
**Transfiguration Day,** nationwide celebrations (6th)

**Feast of the Virgin Mary,** nationwide celebrations (15th)

**International Folklore Festival,** Plovdiv (early in the month)

**International Jazz Festival,** Bansko (around the third week)

**Folklore Festival,** Koprivshtitsa (mid-month)

**Oreshak Annual Fair** (mid-month)

**Shumen Folklore Festival** (all month)

**Sofia International Folklore Festival** (late in the month)

**Pirin Sings,** Bansko (held mid-month in odd-numbered years)

**International Film Festival,** Varna (one week either late August or early September)

**International Folklore Festival,** Burgas (late in the month)

**Watermelon Festival,** Shumen (last Sun)

## September

**Rozhen Fair** (8th)

**Apollonia Arts Festival,** Sozopol. Live concerts around the town (first two weeks of the month)

**Sofia Fest,** held in the capital (15th–18th) around St Sofia's Day, September 17th

**International Plovdiv Fair** (one week late in the month)

## October

**Days of Ruse,** a programme of theatre, music and dance (first two weeks of the month)

**Grape Festival,** Melnik. To celebrate the harvest (early in the month)

## December

**St Nikolai's Day,** nationwide celebrations (6th)

**Young Wine Festival,** Sandanski. First tasting of the year's pressing (early in the month)

**Christmas Fair,** Ruse (15th–24th)

---

**Super-Fest!**
The largest of Bulgaria's festivals is the internationally recognised Koprivshtitsa Folk Festival; however, it is only held every five years (next in 2005, then in 2010). The website *www.balkanfolk.com/events* will keep you up to date with folklore festivals in Bulgaria and the greater Balkan region.

---

Festivals keep the country's song and dance traditions alive

The Bulgarians had lived under Ottoman domination for over 300 years. Their religion, customs, lifestyle and language had all been suppressed. The essence of Bulgarian religious orthodoxy and culture survived in remote monasteries, kept alive by a small number of monks; the heart of Bulgar/Slav identity seemed to have been lost in the mists of time.

However, in the mid 1700s a monk named Paisii Hilendarski set about compiling the first history of the Balkan region – putting into words the heroic feats of Asparukh, the first Bulgarian Tsar, Boris, who unified the people under Christianity, and Simeon, who ruled during a period before the

first millennium when the Empire was at its zenith. The tome was completed in 1762 but even then, had it rested on some dusty library shelf it might have become simply another academic thesis. However, Hilendarski set out on the 18th-century equivalent of a promotional tour and his book caught the public imagination.

The seeds of a renewed identity began to take root just as the shackles of Ottoman rule began to weaken. Orthodoxy emerged from the shadows, the Bulgarian language began to be taught in newly opened schools and a generation of Bulgarians took over the mantle of trade and industry from a declining Turkish mercantile class. This new breed of entrepreneur used its wealth to build fine new houses and patronise the arts for the first time in several generations. Bulgarian craftsmen were suddenly in high demand for traditional building and woodcarving and every large Bulgarian town had a gentrified district built in a style known as Bulgarian National Revival. Along with this renewed national confidence came a renaissance of the arts (*see pp20–3*). Homes, public buildings and churches reflect the new aesthetic and artistic ideal.

There are no set architectural rules for National Revival style – unlike say the Georgian neo-classical style of the 1700s in the UK – but the emphasis is on beauty as part of the daily lives of citizens. Large stone mansions stand in voluminous verdant walled gardens. The exterior of the buildings have brightly painted facades, latticework wooden soffits, awnings and balconies. Interior decoration is characterised by intricately carved wooden ceilings, wardrobes and chests and brightly patterned rugs, carpets and cushions.

Among the best places to see National Revival architecture are:

**Koprivshtitsa**, home of the Bulgarian royal family during Ottoman rule (*see p61*)

**Plovdiv** (alongside architecture from many other eras – *see pp87–90*)

**Tryavna,** famed for its woodcarvers (*see p68*)

**Veliko Turnovo,** capital during the Second Bulgarian Empire, renewed in the late 19th century (*see pp70–5*)

**Melnik,** surrounded by the best vineyards in Bulgaria (*see p84*)

**Shiroka Lûka,** in the heart of the Rodopi Mountains (*see p94*)

**Etur,** a recreated artisan village using original 19th-century buildings (*see p58*)

Facing page: traditional door detail
Below left: a typical National Revival window
Below right: renovated building, Koprivshtitsa

# Impressions

## When to Go

Bulgaria calls itself a year-round destination, and it is true that it provides activities throughout the year, but be aware that many attractions and activities are highly seasonal. The Black Sea season lasts from May to October, with an ultra-busy period late June to the end of August. In the winter the coastal resorts are deserted and almost all hotels are closed.

The skiing season runs from December to April, though there's often enough snow left in May to enjoy a few runs, especially in Bansko (which has the best snow record). Most package tours to the ski resorts stop just after Easter, so you'll need to travel independently to ski after that date.

Hiking can commence in the mountains almost as soon as the snows have melted, and stops as the snows arrive. It can be hot for walking in July and August, but spring and autumn are ideal seasons. The same is true for general touring or visits to the capital.

Most of Bulgaria enjoys a covering of snow in the winter, and because it sits at the boundary between two massive weather systems it can be prone to extremes of every condition. Impressive thunderstorms can happen at all times of year and rain is also a year-round possibility.

Organised excursions are plentiful and a trouble-free way to sightsee outside main towns

Modern Sofia

## Areas to Visit

Because Bulgaria is a multi-dimensional destination, you've got lots of options on where to visit. The Black Sea is an obvious attraction to beach lovers and families, while the mountains offer endless outdoor pursuits and fantastic landscapes. Although the capital Sofia would never claim to have the historical sights of Prague, for instance, it is a likeable city still operating at a people-friendly level and you'll find some exceptional highlights. It's certainly an interesting city-break destination.

For general sightseeing, Bulgaria is a compact country and there's something remarkable in every region, whether it be an impressive monastery, a historic village, mineral springs or traditional artisans. You could easily combine some or all of these into a two-week holiday, or spend longer and savour your favourites.

## How to Get Around

Bulgaria has limited domestic air services because the distances are not great, the infrastructure is too expensive and the demand isn't there. The only viable route is the Sofia/Black Sea service and you can travel all year round to Varna and Burgas, with more services running May–October only.

Trains are a good way to get to the main cities and towns. It's possible to tour from Sofia to Plovdiv, Veliko Turnovo, Ruse, Varna and Burgas on trains of reasonable quality, but it does mean that many of the country's most interesting sites (certainly the monasteries and most of the mountains) will be out of reach.

Really the only way to see the best of what Bulgaria has to offer is to take to the roads. This is a bit of a 'Catch 22', since the roads are generally in poor condition but those willing to drive

Bulgaria is a relaxed and people-friendly country

(with care) will reap major rewards, because then small villages and quiet mountain footpaths are yours to explore.

If you don't want to drive, chartering a car with driver, or a taxi, for the day is an affordable option. This way someone else is taking the strain of driving but you still control the itinerary and time. This could easily be combined with train travel, so that you use major towns as a base to explore by charter vehicle. Alternatively, take a coach tour to the various attractions. The disadvantage of this is you hand over control of the visit to your tour guide.

**What to Wear**

Layering is the byword here. Summer temperatures reach the mid 30°C, so light cotton or breathable clothing is advised, but even in August if you

intend to head to the hills it's wise to carry a warm layer (a fleece is ideal). Spring and autumn could still be warm, so keep the light cotton outfits, but a couple of warmer layers, especially for the fresher evenings, and even one cold weather option should be part of your wardrobe. In the winter months warm and waterproof clothing are a must throughout the country but especially in the mountains.

If you are going to be doing a lot of hiking then specialist boots are advised. Ski equipment can be rented in the resort but you'll need your own ski-suit (or separate jacket and trousers) for the slopes.

A special word about monasteries. The Bulgarian monasteries are not as strict as their Greek counterparts in enforcing a dress code. Shorts and vests seem not to be a problem. However, it is still wise to wear, or carry with you, items of clothing that will cover the thighs and shoulders. Remember these are supposed to be spiritual places where the demure dress of the monks should be a pointer to your own clothing.

## Culture Shock
### Red Tape
Foreigners must register with the police during their stay in Bulgaria. If you are staying in a hotel this will be done for you and you will receive a document from the hotel to confirm your stay. This document must be handed to the customs officer when you leave the country. You must have documentation to cover each night of your stay, so if you are touring around make sure that each hotel provides one.

### Cyrillic
In addition to the usual foreign words encountered in a new overseas holiday destination, you've got a whole new alphabet to get to grips with! Thank St Cyril for that (*see p16*). However, in Sofia and on the Black Sea you'll see numerous helpful signs showing the Roman equivalent spellings on road signs and English menus in restaurants, and as Bulgaria moves closer to joining the EU (scheduled for 2007), more and more roads will be signposted in both the Cyrillic and Roman scripts for towns and villages.

Most people working in the tourist industry will speak some English, but it's a little more challenging in the countryside where, at present, you'll need to brush up on your body language to navigate successfully.

To try to ease your way, throughout this book we show the place names in Cyrillic in brackets but a correct phonetic pronunciation in Roman letters first, so if you are asking directions to a place you'll at least be saying it correctly even if you can't recognise it written in Cyrillic.

You'll find that maps, road signs and guidebooks don't have standard Roman spellings for many towns – this is because it's difficult to translate the sounds of some Cyrillic letters directly into English – particularly Б. This letter is pronounced as a short 'u' in English but is often spelt as 'a' or 'â' on maps – eg. Veliko Târnovo as opposed to Veliko Turnovo.

For more details about spelling and pronunciation see the Language section (*pp182–3*).

Many signs are now in Roman and Cyrillic script

Restaurant menus can be a challenge

## Dual pricing

Although Bulgaria is a cheap destination to visit, it's become common practice in hotels and some restaurants to charge foreigners a different (higher) rate. Bulgarians earn a fraction of the average western salary and few get the chance to travel even within their own country, so foreigners are generally considered to be wealthy.

The best way to get a better deal on hotel rooms is to pre-book through a travel agent. Rack rates can be reduced considerably but it obviously means you've got to pre-plan your whole itinerary.

Food is still very good value even when being charged at tourist rates; however, to eat at local prices ask for a menu in Cyrillic, which will show the true price rate, as well as one in English. In the Black Sea resorts restaurant prices can be 50 per cent higher than inland but since few Bulgarians can afford to stay there this isn't dual pricing, it's just the market rate.

## Yes or No?

Bulgarians shake their head for yes and nod for no. This causes a lot of confusion both in terms of their answers to your questions and your reaction to their queries. Think about your natural reaction the question 'Would you like milk with your coffee?' A short nod for yes will result in a black coffee arriving!

To further confuse the issue, many Bulgarians who work or have worked with foreigners will use a nod for yes and shake their head for no because they know that that is the norm for us.

To keep communications clear it's probably better to say *da* (yes) and *ne* (no) rather than use non-verbal communication.

## Remember

There's a lovely tradition throughout the country of posting obituaries outside the houses of the recently bereaved and also in public areas such as town halls and post offices. Although it's not possible to understand the sentiment expressed in Cyrillic, the pictures of the people are fascinating and poignant.

## Smoking

Bulgaria is a smoker's country and there's little concern for non-smokers in restaurants and bars except in the better-class establishments in Sofia. However, during the summer this doesn't cause much problem, as people can eat and drink alfresco.

## Birthdays and Saints' Days

Most Bulgarians are named after an Orthodox saint and people celebrate their annual saint's day with even more gusto than their actual birthday, because Petars, Kirils or Sophias across the country can get together to party.

## Floral Faux Pas

If invited to a Bulgarian home always take a small gift. Flowers are popular but make sure you take a bouquet with an odd number of blooms. Even-numbered bouquets are for funerals only.

## Tourist Information

Official tourist information is poor, with few tourist offices. For background information try these websites.
*www.mfa.government.bg_en* – English-language section of the official government website, with information on visas and formalities.
*www.bulgaria.com* – General information in English on sites and activities.
*www.bulgaria.net* – Canadian site with information on Bulgaria.

### Street Names

The following abbreviations have been used throughout the book.
bul. – bulevard, meaning avenue/boulevard.
pl. – ploshtad, square.
ul. – ulitsa, street.

The pace of life leaves plenty of time for socialising

# Sofia (София)

Set majestically in the lee of the Vitosha Mountains on an elevated plateau, Sofia is the highest capital in Europe. A city of just over a million people, it reflects the turbulent antecedents of the country but also the challenges facing a Bulgaria on the brink of a new era. Here a few horse-drawn carts still vie for road space with brand new BMWs and Mercedes, and at Orthodox churches teenagers in the latest skimpy western fashions beseech the saints in the flickering light of a votive candle.

Banya Bashi mosque

Sofia was founded at a point equidistant between the Black Sea and the Adriatic and thrived as an important staging post on trade routes travelled since antiquity. The earliest settlement on this site was Thracian Serdica. It went though a number of name changes, including Roman Ulpia Serdica and Byzantine Triaditsa, before taking the name Sofia (see p41), probably from the Church of St Sofia (see p41), during the Second Bulgarian Empire (1185–1396). Under Ottoman rule it was a regional administrative headquarters, and then was chosen as capital of the independent country in 1879.

Today the downtown area is compact and eminently walkable. Several wide boulevards radiate out from the central ploshtad Sveta Nedelya, flanked by elegant public buildings such as the National Assembly and Law Courts. Sofia is a city of statues and monuments and it's hard to find a square or road intersection without a plinth, obelisk or statue. Many relate to Bulgaria's gratitude for Russia's help in ousting the Turks from their soil, though native heroes are not forgotten – from Vasil Levski to St Cyril.

Alexander Nevski Church

## Central Sofia

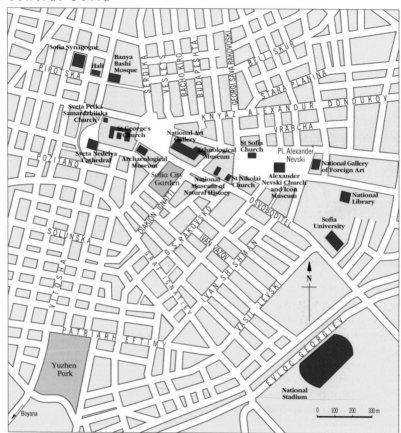

### Alexander Nevski Church
### (Църквата Алежаидър Невски)

Built as a memorial to the over 200,000
Russian troops who perished in the
Russian-Turkish War of 1877–8,
Alexander Nevski is the largest Russian
Orthodox church in the Balkans. Named
after a renowned 13th century Russian
warrior who was the patron saint of Tsar
Alexander II, the church was designed
by Pomerantsev, a noted Russian
religious architect of his day, and
decorated by the finest artists in Europe.
It was completed in 1912.

The edifice is an elegant ensemble of
Romanesque arched window detail,
copper cupolas and gilded domes
offering an ever-changing architectural
line as you view the exterior. The
interior is a vast open space with three
naves. The 52m high dome is supported
by massive columns. Italian marble is
the material predominantly used for
columns, floors and the patriarch's

Sofia Archaeological Museum

throne. The walls are decorated with now-faded murals and the dusty shafts of light from the few windows give the church a rather sober atmosphere.

The crypt of the church now houses the Museum of Icons (*see pp38–9*), *pl. Alexander Nevski. Open 7am–7pm except during services. Admission free, donations welcomed.*

## Archaeological Museum
### (Археологически Музея)
Housed under the domes of the Buyuk Djami (Great Mosque) built in the last decade of the 15th century, the Archaeological Museum is the oldest museum in Bulgaria and opened in 1879. The surprisingly small collection is organised in chronological order and there are good examples of ancient mosaics and Roman statuary, as well as Thracian finds brought from sites across

Bulgaria. The coin collection is one of the finest in the world, with over 150,000 items.
*ul. Tsar Osvoboditel. Tel: (02) 988 24 06. Open Tue–Sun summer 10am–6pm, winter 10.30am–4.30pm. Admission charge.*

## Banya Bashi Mosque
### (Джамията Баня Баши)
The last serving mosque in the city, Banya Bashi was built in the mid 16th century at the height of Ottoman power by the Turkish architect Sinan, the founding father of classical Islamic architecture. It is still used for worship and its singular lack of iconic images offers an interesting contrast to the Orthodox churches in the city.
*Bul. Maria Luisa. Open dawn to dusk except during worship. Admission free.*

**Boyana Church (Бойана Църквата)**
Listed as a World Heritage Site by
UNESCO, tiny Boyana Church houses
what are arguably the finest murals in
the Balkans. The church, set in the
foothills of the Vitosha range in a
southwestern suburb of the city, was
built around 1250 and has almost 100
paintings, the style of which went on to
influence religious art throughout the
region.

The majesty of the murals is
immediately apparent. Rich in their
depth of colour and with a remarkable
lifelike quality in the faces not seen in
European art until the Renaissance 100
years later, the panels in the nave show
the Bulgarian royal family in their fine
robes. Other scenes depict stories from
the Bible and there is an exquisite face of
Christ in the apse cupola.

Work to preserve the original murals
is ongoing and visitors are only allowed
to spend 10 minutes inside the chapel,
so in order to allow more time to study
the detail a Museum of Boyana has been
built next to the church. This displays
copies of many of the finest murals and
shows a short film in English about the
church.
*ul. Boyansko Ezero, Boyana. Church
open Tue–Sun 9am–5.30pm. Admission
charge. Guided tours in English separate
charge. Museum open same hours,
separate admission charge. Bus 64 or
minibus 21.*

Boyana Church

The Ethnological Museum

## Ethnological Museum
### (Етнографски Музея)

Occupying one wing of the imposing former Royal Palace (1893) built in Palladian style but with an Art Nouveau interior, the Ethnological Museum has an exceptional range of Bulgarian arts and crafts dating from around the 1700s to the present day. The galleries here are the perfect place to acquaint yourself with the fine craftsmanship in embroidery, woodcarving, and ceramics before you venture out to buy souvenirs for yourself. Particularly beautiful are the national costumes still worn in so many parts of Bulgaria during folk celebrations. The museum displays illustrate the background to traditional ways of life throughout the country and its major religious festivals.

*pl. Battenberg. Tel: (02) 987 41 92. Open Tue–Sun 10am–5.30pm. Admission charge. Guided tours in English, separate charge.*

## Hali

Built in 1910 in late National Revival style, the Hali is the largest covered market in the city and the place to watch the bustle of everyday life for the citizens of Sofia.
*bul. Maria Luisa, opposite the Banya Bashi Mosque. Open daily 7am–midnight. Admission free.*

## Museum of Icons

This collection of sacred images is Bulgaria's most important and is a must for lovers of religious art.

Housed in the crypt of the Alexander

Nevski Church (*see p35*), the icons date from the 13th to the 19th century, offering a perfect opportunity to explore the subtle changes in style and interpretation in the genre over the centuries. Several major pieces have been rescued from Nesebur (*see pp108–9*) and Sozopol (*see pp112–3*) on the Black Sea, where many churches have fallen into disrepair, whilst others come from monasteries around Bulgaria.
*pl. Alexander Nevski. Tel: (02) 981 57 75. Open Wed–Mon 10.30am–6.30pm. Admission charge. Guided tours in English are available.*

## National Art Gallery
**(Национал Художестранно Галерия)**
Sharing the former Royal Palace with the Ethnological Museum, the National Gallery of Art houses a collection of over 12,000 pieces by 19th and 20th century Bulgarian masters, including many works by the Motev dynasty, who were prolific artists throughout this period. The gallery also has an active programme of temporary exhibitions.
*pl. Battenberg. Tel: (02) 980 00 93. Open Tue–Sun 10.30am–6.30pm. Admission charge, free on Sun. Guided tours in English separate charge. Temporary exhibitions separate charge.*

## National Gallery of Foreign Art
**(Галерия Чуждествена Изкуство)**
The largest gallery in Bulgaria houses an eclectic collection of art from across the globe. It's short on 'recognised' masters, though it does have works by Rembrandt, but the strength of the collection is in its African and Asian

tribal art, which has some exceptionally well-chosen pieces.
*ul. 19 Fevruari, pl. Alexander Nevski. Tel (02) 988 65 30. Open Wed–Mon 11am–6pm. Admission charge, free Sun. Guided tours in English separate charge.*

## National Museum of History
**(Национален Исторически Музей)**
Housed in the former Zhivkov presidential palace, this museum brings together the many strands of Bulgaria's complicated past. The vast collection has been gathered from sites across the country.

The galleries have permanent exhibitions starting with Thracian treasures and then moving on to Roman artefacts found principally at Varna and Veliko Turnovo. Later exhibits shed light on Ottoman rule – including religious persecution and political life – and the role of Russia in Bulgarian Independence in the late 19th century. Of course the Bulgarian National Revival period is not forgotten, with exceptional arts and crafts displays. Throughout the permanent galleries you'll find captioning in English but not much on the background detail, which is only in Cyrillic.

The third floor of the palace holds temporary exhibitions allowing study of different aspects of Bulgarian history in more depth, but captions are generally not in English.
*Residence Boyana, bul. Okolovrusten Pat, Boyana. Tel: (02) 955 42 80. Open daily 9.30am–6pm. Admission charge, free Tue. Guided tours in English, separate charge. Bus 63, 64 or minibus 21.*

Sofia City Garden

## National Museum of Natural History (Национален Мрироодоначен Музей)

The height of fashion throughout Victorian Europe, this collection of what is said to be over a million specimens of minerals, flora and fauna is now considered rather old-fashioned, but kids will find the stuffed animals and live creepy crawlies in jars much more fascinating than magnificent icons or Roman artefacts in other museums, and it certainly is extensive.

*bul. Tsar Osvoboditel. Tel: (02) 988 51 51. Open daily 10am–6pm. Admission charge.*

## Roman Remains

There are tantalising glimpses of the old Sofia in a couple of locations in the city. Behind Banya Bashi Mosque is the most imposing, the walls of a 6m brick turret from the fort of Ulpia Serdica, built in the 3rd century AD but renovated during the second Bulgarian Empire.

Several metres of wall have also been preserved in the underpass opposite the presidency, showing Roman and Byzantine levels.

## Sofia City Garden

Right in the heart of town, tiny Sofia City Garden (Gradanskata Gradina Park, Граданската Градина Парк) is where locals like to take time out during the day to read a book, eat lunch or simply relax; you'll usually find groups of retired men playing chess and passing the time and there are one or two cafés where you can take coffee.

*Between bul. Tsar Osvoboditel and bul. General Gurko at ul. Battenberg. Open 24 hours.*

## St George's Church
### (Църквата Св Георги)

The oldest extant building in Sofia, St George's church was erected as a secular rotunda by the Romans in the 2nd century BC. It was converted into a Christian place of worship sometime during the early Middle Ages and then into a mosque during the Ottoman era. Damaged during the Second World War, it was rebuilt and renovated in the late first millennium Romanesque style. The earliest wall murals in the interior date from the 10th century.

*Behind the Sheraton Hotel. Open summer 8am–6pm, winter 8am–5pm. Admission free, donations welcomed.*

## St Sofia Church (Църквата Св София)

The city's patron and namesake St Sofia is venerated at this 6th-century Byzantine church erected during the reign of the Emperor Justinian, who also supervised the building of the great St Sophia church in Constantinople (now Istanbul). The church was the centre of Orthodox worship during the second Bulgarian Empire but the Ottomans added minarets during the 1400s, after they took control of the area. Following damage during a series of earthquakes the church was totally rebuilt at the start of the 20th century, and curiously it kept its minarets during the rebuilding even though the Ottomans had lost power in the area. Few of the wall frescoes have survived but the church does own a lock of the hair of pre-eminent Bulgarian freedom fighter Vasil Levski (*see p78*).

Sofia City Garden's cafés offer a welcome break from sightseeing

Sveta Nedelya Cathedral

*ul. Panzh, pl. Alexander Nevski.*
*Open summer 7am–7pm, winter*
*7am–6pm except during services.*
*Admission free, donations welcomed.*

## St Nikolai (Russian) Church
(Църквата Св Николай)

Funded by Russian émigrés in the years
just before the Revolution (1912), this
archetypal Orthodox church built by
Russian artisans from the Moscow
School of Decorative Arts is one of the
landmarks of Sofia. Though the highly
coloured ornate exterior is much
photographed, the highlights lie within
the recently renovated interior, with
frescoes from the Novgorod School. The
icon of St Nikolai Chudotvorets is
revered as 'the wonder worker' and
you'll find a steady stream of
worshippers humbly requesting his help.
*ul. Tsar Osvoboditel. Open 7am–7pm*
*except during services. Admission free,*
*donations welcomed.*

## Sveta Nedelya Cathedral
(Катедралата Св Неделя)

The symbol of Sofia, sitting at the very
heart of the city, the cathedral was
completed in 1863 on foundations from
the Middle Ages but completely
destroyed in a bomb blast in 1925 (an
unsuccessful attempt on the life of King
Boris III, who was worshipping there,
though it killed 120 other worshippers).
The church was rebuilt in neo-

Romanesque style with an exceptionally ornate interior but the highlights are the icons painted by Stanislav Dospevski, a Bulgarian artist born in Pazardzhik. Sveta Nedelya is one of the busiest churches in the capital, as workers call in at lunchtime or between meetings to light a candle and say a prayer. It is fascinating to see young and old, rich and poor alike keeping the Orthodox faith alive.

*pl. Sveta Nedelya, at the corner of buls Vitosha and Stamboliiski.*
*Open 7am–7pm except during services. Admission free, donations welcomed.*

### Sveta Petka Samardzhiiska Church (Църквата Св Петка Самарджийска)

From ground level only the terracotta tiles of the roof of Sveta Petka Samardzhiiska Church (Church of St Peter of the Saddle Makers) are visible. It was a Christian place of worship built during the early years of Ottoman rule, explaining its low position and rather humble exterior. You can reach the church from the pedestrian underpass that runs under Nezavisimost Square where it meets pl. Sveta Nedelya.

While the exterior of the church was designed to be as plain as possible, the interior was a riot of bright murals depicting scenes from the New Testament. Today, though they have lost much of their lustre, they form an important example of how Orthodoxy was sustained under Muslim rule.
*Pl. Sveta Nedelya. Open 7am–7pm. Admission charge.*

### Sofia Synagogue

One of only a handful of synagogues in Bulgaria and the largest in the country, the Sofia synagogue was completed in 1910. A small museum tracing the history of the Jews in Bulgaria has useful captions in English and there is an interesting visit with an English-speaking guide. There are no set opening hours, so just knock at the door to see if a visit is possible.
*Ul. Ezerh Yosif. No set opening hours. Admission charge.*

### Yuzhen Park (Юзен Парк)

Situated southwest of the town centre, Yuhzen Park is another place where city dwellers come to relax. It's a good place to bring children, as there's a funfair with rides, and it's a great place to meet Bulgarian families, especially at weekends and holidays.

The park was planned around the imposing NDK National Palace of Culture, Bulgaria's largest arts/entertainment and exhibition venue (*see Entertainment, p152*) with 16 separate halls and theatres. Designed in sombre 'socialist' style, it was opened in 1981.

Yuzhen has two memorials of interest. The monumental 1300 Anniversary Monument, erected in 1981 to commemorate the founding of the First Bulgarian Empire, is now a crumbling wreck surrounded by a high fence to stop people getting injured. Much more evocative is the memorial to those who died at the hands of the communist regime. A simple wall of marble etched with the names of the lost stands next to a tiny chapel.
*Corner of bul. Maria Luisa and bul. Patriarh Evtimii. Open 24 hours.*

# Walk: Central Sofia

Central Sofia is very compact and you'll be able to take in many of the major sights on the route of this 2.5km walk. How long it takes really depends on how long you spend admiring the churches or how interesting you find the museums, but allow 2 hours for the walk itself. You won't be short of cafés en route, so there's plenty of opportunity for refreshments.

*Start at the central hub of the town, pl. Sveta Nedelya (пл света Недалйа), one of the busiest parts of the city for traffic and people.*

## 1 Sveta Nedelya Cathedral

The cathedral sits of the heart of the square. Completed in 1863, it had to be rebuilt in 1925 following a bomb attack. *Leave the square by taking the underpass under pl. Nezavisimost (пл Независимост), keeping the Sheraton Hotel immediately to your right. You'll*

*find Sveta Petka Samardzhiiska Church here, sitting incongruously in the shadow of the contemporary city.*

## 2 Sveta Petka Samardzhiiska Church

This Orthodox church was built during the early years of Ottoman rule in the 14th century. It had to be inconspicuous so as not to compete with the mosques of the city. The interior has some splendid murals.
*Retrace your steps back to pl. Sveta Nedelya and leave by ul. Saborna*

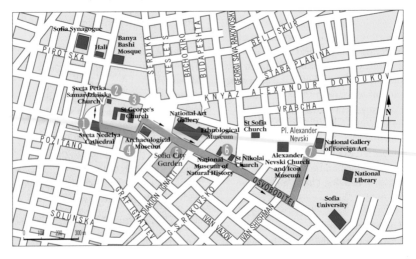

(ул савориа) *(keeping the Sheraton building on your left). Take the first left into the quadrangle behind the hotel to find St George's Church.*

## 3 St George's Church

This is the oldest building in Sofia, built as a rotunda by the Romans and converted into a church in the early Christian era. The earliest murals inside date from the 10th century.

*Return to ul. Saborna and continue for the short distance to its intersection with ul. Lege* (ул Леге)*, where you'll see the Archaeological Museum across the street to your left.*

## 4 Archaeological Museum

This interesting collection of ancient artefacts is housed in the Great Mosque, built in the late 1400s.

*From the entrance of the museum turn right into pl. Battenberg* (пл Баттенберг) *but if it's close to the hour wait here to see the changing of the guard at the presidential offices on the far side of ul. Lege.*

## 5 Ploshtad Battenberg

Battenberg Square (though it's hardly discernable as a square in the true sense) is the heart of 'Third Empire' Sofia, totally redesigned when the city became capital of a newly independent Bulgaria. Sofia City Garden lies on the right after the imposing central bank building. This is a good place to stop for a coffee. On the left is the long elegant façade of the former Royal Palace, now the Ethnological Museum and the National Art Gallery.

*From the museum/gallery entrance turn*

*left, leaving the square along bul. Tsar Osvoboditel* (бул Цаз Освободител)*. At the intersection of ul. Rakovski* (ул Ракобски) *150m further on is St Nikolai Church.*

## 6 St Nikolai Church

This colourful Russian Orthodox church was built by Russian émigrés in the years just before the Revolution but its ornate interior is furnished with many earlier icons.

*From the church, turn left along ul. Rakovski. One hundred metres further on, on the right pl. Alexander Nevski* (пл Алежандег невски) *comes into view.*

## 7 Ploshtad Alexander Nevski

This is one of the finest vistas in the city. Behind the activity of the daily collectors' market, the copper and gold domes of Alexander Nevski Church rise majestically, framed by an avenue of trees. On the left of the square as you walk towards the church is the tomb of the Unknown Soldier, while behind this is St Sofia Church, built in the 6th century.

### The Battenbergs

Because the Bulgarians hadn't had royal rulers since 1396 there was no strong bloodline to claim the throne. Alexander Battenberg was a German Prince (the Battenberg family originated in Hesse), elected to the Bulgarian throne with the title of Prince. The Battenbergs were well connected with most royal houses in Europe, including the Russian, Greek and British Royal families. Because of anti-German feeling during the First World War the British branch changed their surname to the more English-sounding Mountbatten. Prince Philip, Queen Elizabeth II's consort, is the most famous Mountbatten today.

# Excursions from Sofia

Sofia is blessed with a delightful selection of attractions just on the doorstep. Less then an hour by car from the capital you can find 'Bulgaria in microcosm,' magnificent nature in the form of mountain landscapes, lakes and gorges; cultural and historical sites; and the opportunity to enjoy a variety of outdoor pursuits.

Vitosha National Park chairlift

## Vitosha National Park
## (Национален Парк Витоша)

Twenty-two thousand hectares of protected mountains overlook Sofia, pressing into the suburbs of the capital. Vitosha is the capital dwellers'

Mountain café, Vitosha National Park

playground and is known by everyone as 'the lungs of the city'. They flock to the slopes for winter skiing, summer hiking, or to simply escape the urban smog – especially at weekends, when the city is empty but Vitosha is packed with Bulgarians enjoying family picnics or romantic trysts.

That said, on weekdays there are opportunities to enjoy more peace and quiet, and if you are on a short break to Sofia rather than touring the whole country, a trip to Vitosha gives you an impression of what you are missing – majestic landscapes – plus panoramic long-range views of the city in the valley below.

Strangely, although it gives its name to the park Mount Vitosha is not the highest peak in the mountain range. That accolade goes to Mount Cherni Vruh (The Black Mount), at 2290m the fourth highest in the country. The mountain suffers from cloud cover on average 250 days a year, so don't be surprised if it's not visible during your stay. A feature of the range are the *moreni*, 'rivers of stone', which are characterised by huge granite boulders filling the river valleys; they were carried down the mountain aeons ago by

## Sofia Environs

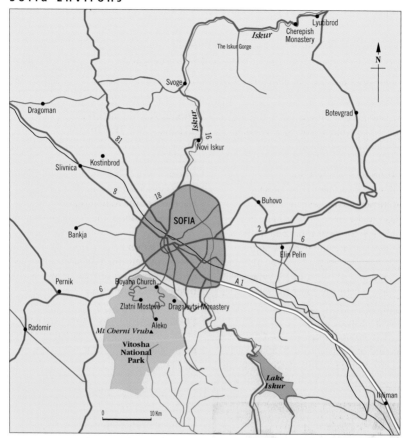

glaciers that melted at the end of the Ice Age and deposited them here.

The upper elevations of the park are accessible by car on its northern side but it's much easier to take either the (2-person open) chairlift from Dragalevtsi (Драгалевци) (bus services from the Hladinika bus station) or the gondola (6-person enclosed) from Simeonovo (Симеоново) (bus services also from the Hladinika bus station), both on the lower slopes just outside the city.

### Aleko (Алеко)

There's little more in this tiny resort than a handful of cafés/restaurants and a couple of rather tired-looking hotels; however, Aleko (1800m) is a terminus for one of the Vitosha chairlifts and the end point of one of the roads into the National Park. It's a popular starting point for summer hikes and climbs, and winter skiing, including the longest cross-country skiing trail in the country. From here it's a gruelling 90-minute climb to the summit of Cherni Vruh (though you can take the chairlift to Maluk Rezen, from where it's a less strenuous 30-minute route).

**Zlatni Mostove (Златни Мостове)**
This small mountain settlement lies on the northern slopes of the Vitosha range. Its name means 'golden bridges', a reference to the gold panning that used to take place in the river here. Some say that it's still possible to spot the odd fleck shining in the sandy shallows, so you may be able to profit from your trip!

Zlatni Mostove is famed for its *moreni*, impressive gigantic granite glacial boulders that are now blanketed in a veneer of moss, which smother the course of the River Boyana.

A footpath links Boyana Church (*see p37*) with Zlatni Mostove. Some sections are steep and the route should take around 5 hours on a round trip. (*Bus 261 from Hladinika bus station, Sofia.*)

**Dragalevtsi Monastery (Драгалевци Манастир)**
Dragalevtsi was erected in around 1350 and was once one of 14 that dotted Vitosha, collectively known as the Mala Sveta Gora ('little Mount Athos' – a reference to the holy collection of monasteries on Mount Athos in Greece). A hotbed of dissent during the 17th century, it became a hideout for Bulgarian freedom fighters, playing host to Vasil Levski for many months. Much of the early complex has been lost

Lake Iskur is a magnet for watersports enthusiasts

during battles with the Turks but the
church has some interesting murals
dating from the1460s.
*(Buses 64 and 93 from Hladinika bus
station, Sofia.)*

### Lake Iskur (Язовир Искър)

The damming of the River Iskur (also
spelled Iskâr on many maps) has created
this huge artificial lake 40km to the
southeast of the city, which acts as a
magnet for watersports enthusiasts. To
find the lake simply follow the
numerous vehicles sporting windsurfers
or pulling trailers carrying kayaks and
canoes.

A few enterprising businesses have
sprung up renting equipment to tourists
or Bulgarians who don't own their own,
but this is an industry that has plenty of
capacity for development. Many non-
sporting city dwellers head to Lake Iskur
for a long lunch on the sunny terrace of
one of the many lakeside restaurants,
where freshwater lake trout is often on
the menu.

Lake Iskur fishermen

### The Iskur Gorge (Ишкар)

Though the River Iskur circumvents the
capital, the path of the river north of
Sofia has some exceptional natural
features. The gorge stretches 156
kilometres, but by far the best stretch
lies between Svoge and Lyutibrod, less
than 40km from the capital. The sheer
walls of granite rise over 100m above
the river valley, sheltering a series of
pretty agricultural villages. The karst
landscape has created several large caves,
the spectacular 80m Skaklya Waterfall,
and the naturally eroded Kutinski
Pyramids just north of Novi Iskur.

It plays host to several monasteries,
including Cherepish (*see p124*) and the
Sedemte Prestola Monastery, founded in
the 11th century, the church of which is
unique in Bulgaria in having seven naves
and iconostases (three flanking each side
of the main nave).

### It's a Date

The birth of the Bulgarian sport of hiking
began on 27th August 1895, when
Bulgarian writer and philosopher Aleko
Konstantinov invited the population of Sofia
to join him in a mass walk from the city
centre to the summit of Mount Cherni Vruh
(2290m). Over 300 people turned out in
what must have seemed a rather eccentric
excursion but it started a trend that soon
became the height of fashion.

# Drive: Around Vitosha National Park

This full-day (8-hour) excursion allows you to leave central Sofia and enjoy some of the historical and natural attractions just on the doorstep of the city. You could combine it with a hike in Vitosha National Park, as there are many easy footpaths that don't require specialist footwear. If you do, it's sensible to carry a warmer/waterproof layer in case the weather changes.
*Distance: 260km.*

*Set out from Sofia down the arterial route heading southwest (bul. Makedonika/Македоника becomes bul. Totleden/Тотлоден then turns into bul. Tsar Boris III/Цар Борис) in the direction of Kulata (Кулата). At the intersection with the Sofia Ring Road (bul. Nikola Petka/Никола Петко) approximately 5km from the city centre turn left in the direction of Plovdiv (Пловдив) then 750m later turn right on ul. Alexander Pushkin (ул Александер Пущкин).*

*After another kilometre a small maze of streets hides Boyana Church (ask for directions to the Boyana Museya).*

## 1 Boyana Church

This tiny UNESCO listed church has some of the most remarkable medieval frescoes in the Orthodox world, but you must visit the interior, as the exterior is of rather uninspiring plain brick.
*Retrace your route back to the Ring Road and turn left. Immediately on your right you'll find the old Presidential Residence set in verdant parkland.*

## 2 Presidential Residence

The palace now houses Bulgaria's premier museum, the National Museum of History. Within the museum there is a vast collection of ancient artefacts and culturally important pieces reflecting every aspect of Bulgaria's complicated past.
*Continue on the Ring Road, still in the direction of Plovdiv. Four kilometres on from the museum you'll come to a*

*crossroads; take a right, signposted Dragalevtsi (Драгалевци) and Aleko (Алеко). The road leads through Dragalevtsi village and past the Dragalevtsi chairlift (if you don't want to drive up the hill then take this scenic open lift) and then begins to climb out of the valley up towards Aleko.*

### 3 Aleko

As the road twists and turns you'll get exceptional views back down over Sofia on the plateau below. Finally after 7km you will arrive at the end of the road (literally) and the small car park at Aleko. There are several rustic cafés here and marked (well worn) footpaths across the hills.

*From Aleko wend your way back to the Ring Road. Take a left again, continuing to follow signs for Plovdiv. After 10km another crossroads offers a right turn on the A82 in the direction of Samokov (Самоков). Take this turn and follow the road 27km to Lake Iskur.*

### 4 Lake Iskur

This man-made expanse was created when the River Iskur was barraged, and it's now a watery playground for the city dwellers. It's difficult to get good views across the lake. The best way is to stop at a roadside restaurant for coffee or a late lunch.

*From here it's only a further 30km to Borovets (Боровец) through the town of Samokov (15km).*

### 5 Borovets

Borovets is Bulgaria's premier ski resort but it's worth a visit at any time of year. In summer, you can stroll around the compact centre perusing the souvenir stalls, hike in the hills, hire a horse for a cross-country trek or enjoy some refreshment on the terrace of a café at the bottom of the pistes.

*From Borovets, return to Sofia, carrying on across the Ring Road to return to the downtown area via bul. Tsarigradsko Shose (бул Цариградско Шосе).*

Lake Iskur roadside restaurant

# Drive: The Iskur Gorge

This impressive natural gorge lies less than an hour from central Sofia. The views are dramatic but are matched by the traditional rural lifestyles in the villages along the valley floor. If you have packed your crampons and pitons, this is the place to try your hand at mountaineering – on the challenging, precipitous gorge walls.

*Time: 6 hours. Distance: 125km.*

*Head north out of Sofia on bul. Rozhen (бул Рожен) in the direction of Novi Iskur and Ruse. You'll pass one of the city's major markets on your left on the outskirts when bul. Rozhen becomes route 16. You'll soon leave the city behind and find yourself in a shallow valley where the major occupation is agriculture.*

*Small farms and old-style methods can still be seen here with many horse-drawn carts and ploughs. You'll pick up the River Iskur 3km south of Novi Iskur, then you'll find yourself in the town proper.*

## 1 Novi Iskur (Нови Искър)

Novi Iskur is the gateway to the gorge. From here you can walk an hour and a half west to the Kutinski Pyramids, an unusual natural rock formation caused by erosion. It's also possible to drive to the region of the pyramids in about 20 minutes.

*Beyond Novi Iskur the rolling topography continues. The road and river now shadow each other along the valley floor, vying for space with the railway line. A bright modern sign in Roman lettering announces your arrival in Svoge (40km north of Sofia).*

## 2 Svoge (Свoге)

This town of around 10,000 inhabitants sits at the confluence of the rivers Iskur and Iskretsa. It has a small history museum and St Paraskeva Church, with some interesting 17th-century murals.

*Beyond Svoge the gorge presents the most dramatic side of its personality. The river is flanked by sheer walls of grey limestone some 100m high, twisting lithely along the tortured path of the river (better on the left bank than the right). This region plays host to a magical wonderland of springs, caves and jagged peaks, the rocky curtains cutting north along several tributaries. Stop at the villages of Bov, Lakatnik and Opletnya.*

### 3 Bov (Бов)

Stop at the village of Bov to find the footpath that leads to Skaklya Waterfall, one of the highest in the country. The route is well marked from the railway station.

### 4 Lakatnik (Лакатник)

The village has one of the country's most famous formations, the Lakatnik Rocks – birthplace of Bulgarian mountaineering.

### 5 Opletnya (Оплетня)

Opletnya is famed for its sheep's cheese and now has a plant producing Bulgarian 'yellow cheese' – the ingredient on many a Bulgarian pizza! A kilometre beyond the village there's a turning right to the village of Elenovdol. The Sedemte Prestola Monastery sits high in the Balkan Peaks off this road at the end of a three-hour walk.
*Road conditions deteriorate around Zverino – though they are pretty average for the rest of Bulgaria. 10km beyond Zverino you'll find a small battered signpost to Cherepish Monastery (left and then 500m down a track).*

The Iskur Gorge offers dramatic views from the road

### 6 Cherepish Monastery (Черепишки Манастир)

Cherepish is evocatively set on a narrow valley by the river in a cleft in the jagged white cliffs. It's almost invisible from the main road and it's like a world apart. Geese, ducks and piglets roam free just outside the monastery complex. Apart from the occasional sounds of road traffic it could almost be the 18th century rather than the 21st! (*see also p124*).
*Returning to the road, the river valley widens out and the valley is once again given over to agriculture as Mezdra approaches. Don't make a detour to this industrial town (the largest railway junction in the country). Instead travel north to Vratsa and take coffee in one of the cafés on ul. Hristo Botev before returning to Sofia.*

# Central Bulgaria

Dominated by the eastern Balkan Mountains, also known as the Stara Planina range, central Bulgaria has always been the core of the country, both geographically and culturally. Two old Bulgarian capitals can be found here, along with a handful of traditional villages preserved as living museums, where you'll be able to stroll around some of the finest National Revival architecture in the country.

Arbanasi handicrafts

In this heartland of Bulgarian nationalism many towns proudly remember their native sons lost in the fight for freedom. The monasteries nestling in remote valleys lent their

Souvenir stall, Arbanasi

support to the nationalists but their exceptional mural decoration is what draws non-Bulgarian tourists.

### Arbanasi (Арбанаси)

One of the architectural highlights of central Bulgaria, Arbanasi is now a village but was once much larger; granted exemption from all taxation by Süleyman I in the 1530s, it grew wealthy from Ottoman trade. Bulgaria's upper echelons were drawn here throughout the 17th and 18th centuries, building expansive mansions, but most of these were destroyed during raids by Turkish bandits. Today the remaining buildings, and a handful of the 90 churches erected in Arbanasi, have been protected under Bulgarian law. Renovation work is an ongoing process but you'll see many fine completed examples – strong stone houses and large gardens set in high stone walls. A number of Revival buildings have been transformed into charming boutique hotels, making Arbanasi a relaxing place to stay and an alternative to the limited choice at Veliko Turnovo (*see pp70–5*).

Konstantsaliev House is an excellent National Revival mansion built on earlier foundations. The upper floors are furnished in period style with original pieces while there is a small gift shop on the ground floor. (*No street address; open daily 9am–5pm; admission charge.*)

Arbanasi's Rozhdesto Hristovo (Nativity) Church is the oldest remaining in the town. The interior design is unusual as it features separate sections for the sexes but the church is renowned for its decoration, including splendid murals of The Last Judgement and The Nativity, both completed in 1597, and the fine iconostasis carved by master craftsmen from Tryavna (*see pp68–9*).

Archangels St Michael and Gabriel's Church in the southeast of the village was built in three phases between the mid 16th and late 18th centuries. Its murals show a development in style over the period.

*5km northwest of Veliko Turnovo. Bus connections with Veliko Turnovo from the main road 400m from the village.*

A picturesque well in Arbanasi

### The Beautiful Bulgaria Project

Since the fall of communism the Bulgarian authorities have embarked on an ambitious programme to renovate its shabby, neglected National Revival architecture. The old quarters of many towns and villages have taken advantage of generous grants to save these beautiful buildings.

## Central Bulgaria

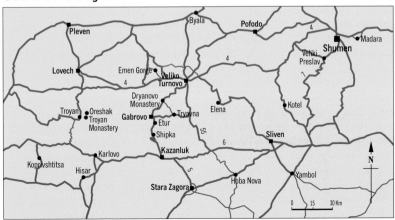

Dryanovo Monastery

## Dryanovo Monastery
### (Дряновски Манастир)

Founded in the 12th century under sheer limestone bluffs next to a river, Dryanovo is most famed for its role in the fight for Bulgarian freedom. Before the Russian-Turkish War (1877–78) it was a main hideout for the Haidouks (*see pp78–9*), including Vasil Levski, and during the war it became a battleground as local people fought with Turkish forces bent on wholesale slaughter. The Bulgarians were unsuccessful, not helped by an accidental explosion of their gunpowder stock, and many died as Ottoman forces stormed the complex. A small mausoleum at the site marks the event and the monks will happily point out the damage done to the Holy Archangel St Michael Church during the attack; the church was less than 20 years old at the time. It has just undergone a major renovation to bring its frescoes back to the brilliant colours they dsplayed when they had just been completed. For this reason it is certainly worth visiting to see how the frescoes in all the monastery churches would have looked when freshly painted.

For more background on the role of Dryanovo during the Russian-Turkish War visit the Komplex Bodopadi next door, where there is a small museum relating to the uprising (*admission charge*).

The new Dryanovo ecotrail offers a marked walking route through the countryside around the monastery and you can explore Bacho Kiro Cave, one of the largest in the country.

*Open daily 8am–8pm. Admission free. 5km from the village of Dryanovo, 25km south of Veliko Turnovo. Bus connections from Veliko Turnovo to the turn-off on the main road. Then 500m walk to the monastery.*

## Elena (Елена)

One of the least known of Bulgaria's 'living museums,' Elena possesses exceptional National Revival architecture including the National Revival Complex around the Church of the Assumption, a collection of 19th century buildings (*open daily 9am–noon and 2pm–5pm; admission charge*), and Daskalolivnitsa, the first teacher training complex in Bulgaria, opened in 1844, which now hosts a museum charting the development of the village (*open daily 9am–noon and*

*2pm–5pm; admission charge).*
*40km southeast of Veliko Turnovo. Bus*
*connections with Sliven, Stara Zagora and*
*Veliko Turnovo.*

## Emen Gorge (Емен)

Three kilometres long and 30m high,
Emen Gorge cuts into the Stara Planina
hills on their northern side. The village
of Emen itself is a typical agricultural
settlement and there are no signs to the
gorge. Park your car close to the old
wooden bridge (take a right once you
cross the river) and a footpath leads up
through the fields to the gorge mouth.
In a totally unspoilt ecosystem, you'll be
surrounded by butterflies and crickets,
along with several hundred other species
of insects, as you walk along the

footpath. Frogs call loudly from pools
gouged over the aeons by the stream
running through the gorge floor and up
on the left side of the cliff at the
entrance is a large cave housing a small
colony of bats.
*30km northwest of Veliko Turnovo.*
*No feasible public transport.*

### The Freedom Fighter's Resolution
'Pasha,
We want the Government to acknowledge
our rights as a people and until this is done
we will not surrender to your tormentors'
hands as long as we are still alive.
We have made our decision to die and we
shall keep our oath.'
 Rebel leader Bacho Kiro's reply when he
was asked by Fazlu Pasha to surrender
during the siege of Dryanovo Monastery.

Emen Gorge

Etur Ethnographical Village Museum

## Etur (Етър)

Etur Ethnographical Village Museum (often spelled Etâr or Etâra) is unique in Bulgaria – a theme park, though don't let the use of that phrase conjure up a Disneyland image. This is a faithful reproduction of a 19th-century Bulgarian settlement. The wood and lime plaster buildings, with stone slab roofs in National Revival style, are linked by cobbled alleyways, rebuilt here on this expansive wooded site by the side of a fast-flowing stream.

Etur offers a full range of traditional Bulgarian arts and crafts. Over 50 workshops and studios offer the finest hand-crafted souvenirs and you can watch the craftsmen at work. You'll find artisans such as jewellers, weavers, potters, leather-toolers and glass-blowers, as well as trades including wheelwrights, cobblers and knife-sharpeners working in water-powered mills. Perhaps the most renowned artisan is the icon painter who has developed an international reputation in the use of traditional Bulgarian techniques (*see pp148–9*).

*7km southeast of Gabrovo. Look for a turning to the left just before the road climbs to the Shipka Pass opposite the panel telling you whether the pass is open or not. Website www.etar.hit.bg; open Mon–Fri 9am–6pm, Sat–Sun 9am–5.30pm. Admission charge, tickets valid for the day. Guided tours in English separate charge. Bus connections with Gabrovo.*

## Gabrovo (Габрово)

This rather insignificant little town has earned a reputation as the centre of Bulgarian comedy – for reasons unknown. Its citizens are the butt of many jokes but seem to have taken it in good humour; the town even has a Museum of Humour and Satire (*ul. Bryanska 68; tel: (066) 39322, www.humourhouse.com; open summer daily 9am–6pm, winter Mon–Sat 9am–6pm; admission charge*) where comic works from 153 countries can be viewed. The museum also has a colourful collection of carnival masks from around the world.

*47km north of Kazanluk. Bus connections with Kazanluk, Plovdiv, Ruse, Veliko Turnovo.*

## Hisar (Хисар)

Known for its mineral springs, Hisar (also known as Hisarya/Хисаря) is popular with Bulgarians, who travel here for the restorative treatments (*see pp 164–5*). If this isn't your thing, come to explore the remains of the ancient spa that provided curative therapies for over 1,000 years.

The immense walls are the most obvious feature of the old settlement. Built during the Roman era but fortified by the Byzantines, they stand 5m high and are the most complete in the country. The Archaeological Museum (*ul. Stamboliiski 8; open daily 8am–noon and 1pm–5pm; admission charge*) features a model of Hisar at its zenith, along with displays of local handicrafts

and traditional tools.

*15km southwest of Karlovo. Bus connections with Karlovo, Troyan, Plovdiv and Veliko Turnovo.*

### A Gabrovo Joke!

Here's an example of Gabrovo humour:
'Why are you crying?' the man asks a young child.
'Because my mother gave me a lev and I've lost it' says the boy
'Well here is another lev, you can stop crying now' replies the man. But the child continues to sob.
'What's the matter now?' enquires the man.
'Because if I hadn't lost the first lev, I would have had two now!' retorts the boy.

Hisar's Roman-Byzantine remains

**Karlovo (Карлово)**

Birthplace of Bulgarian hero Vasil Levski (look out for a monumental statue of the man with a lion at his side in pl. Vasil Levski), Karlovo was a prosperous trading town until the Russian-Turkish War, when it was torched by Ottoman forces.

The Vasil Levski House-Museum (*ul. General Kartzov; tel: (0335) 3498; open Mon–Fri 8.30am–1pm and 2pm–5.30pm; admission charge. Guided tours in English, separate charge*) has information in English about Levski and his life. Only the cellar of the house is original, the rest was lost to the fire of 1877 but rebuilt to the original plans in 1937. *50km north of Plovdiv. Bus connections with Hisar, Kazanluk, Sliven, Stara Zagora, Troyan.*

**Kazanluk (Казанлък)**

Kazanluk (often spelled Kazanlâk) is an unprepossessing town set between the Rodopi and Stara Planina ranges. It is famed for its Thracian tomb, built in the 4th century BC. Protected by UNESCO, it is often closed for archaeological study, but don't despair, as you'll find a full-scale replica of the tomb in the gardens on site (*both at Tyulbeto Park. Open daily 8am–6pm; admission charge*). The beehive-shaped dome is 12m in diameter and decorated with fantastic murals depicting funerary rituals. The tomb is reached down an entry corridor flanked by dramatic battle friezes.

To complement the visit, head next to the Iskra Museum (*ul. Sv Kiril & Metodii; open daily 9am–5pm; admission charge*) which exhibits frescoes from the Magli tomb –another Thracian funerary cavern – and an interesting collection of Greek artefacts found in the region.

Kazanluk's position at the eastern end of the Valley of the Roses makes it a suitable place to find the Museum of the Roses (*ul. Osvobozhdenie; open daily 9am–5pm; admission free*) with displays on the techniques for manufacturing natural fragrances; however, explanations are only in Cyrillic. The shop sells some fragrant souvenirs, including rose-scented soaps, oils and perfumes. *40km northwest of Stara*

## VALLEY OF THE ROSES

Until recently Bulgaria produced 70% of the world's rose oil, a vital resource in the perfume and cosmetics industry. In the 17th century, demand for oil from Western Europe and particularly the French perfume industry hit the roof and it became Bulgaria's most important export commodity. Even today high-profile cosmetics houses such a Helena Rubinstein seek out this pure essence and you can buy Bulgarian-made rose souvenirs such as soap, oils and sweets. The modern industry is concentrated in the valley west of Kazanluk.

*Zagora. Bus connections with Lovech, Stara Zagora, Veliko Turnovo.*

## Koprivshtitsa (Копривштица)

A tour de force of Bulgarian National Revival architecture, Koprivshtitsa is a living museum set in a verdant valley in the heart of the Sredna Gora Mountains. In the 15th century this simple farming village was transformed by the arrival of the ruling nobility, who abandoned the capital Veliko Turnovo in the wake of the Ottoman invasion. They built luxurious mansions amongst the woodland here, creating a kind of royal court in waiting that in turn attracted the Bulgarian intellectual and the merchant élite.

It was at Koprivshtitsa that the seeds of Bulgarian discontent bore the fruit of rebellion when the national uprising was announced on Kalachev Bridge on 20th April 1876. The founding of the Bulgarian state proved a mixed blessing for the village. The merchants and intellectuals moved back to the cities, forsaking their mansions, but this has allowed Koprivshtitsa to retain its authentic architecture and its 19th-century ambience.

You'll make the best of your visit by simply wandering as the whim takes you along the cobbled alleyways, the banks of the River Topolnitsa, which runs through the heart of the town, or the several streams that feed it. A number of houses have stories to tell. Oslekov House (*ul. Garanilo*) is a *pièce de*

Koprivshtitsa village

*résistance* of Revival style built in 1856 for a merchant who lost his life in the uprising. The rooms feature period furniture and the paraphernalia of daily life.

Lutov House (also called Topalov House) (*ul. Nikola Belodezhdov*) is another exceptional example, constructed in 1854, with interior frescoes depicting scenes from Venice, Cairo and Istanbul. The lower floors feature a display of articles made from locally fabricated felt, some of which are for sale.

Kableshkov House, completed two decades later, was owned by the man responsible for firing the first shot of the uprising and now houses a museum dedicated to the struggle for independence.

Popular with Bulgarian visitors, Debelyanov House (*ul. Garanilo*) is dedicated to acclaimed poet Dimcho Debelyanov, who lived here before his death during the First World War. Many of his original manuscripts can be viewed; however, it will be the the the house itself that is most interesting to non-Bulgarian visitors.

The huge equestrian statue dominating the hillside above the town is of Georgi Benkovski, leader of the rebel cavalry, who died at the hands of the Turks in 1876. There are excellent views across the valley from here. Benkovski's mansion sits just below the statue.
*110km west of Sofia. Village open 24 hours, admission free. Buildings are open summer daily 9.30am–5.30pm, winter daily 9.30am–5pm. Admission charge is a combined ticket for all houses open to the public. Bus connections with Pirdop 35km away, which has longer-distance services.*

## Kotel (Котел)
Birthplace of revolutionaries Georgi Rakovski and Safronii Vrachanski, Kotel is famed for its woollen carpets, which are still handmade on wooden looms. The Carpet Exhibition Hall or Galatan School (*ul. Izvorska 17; tel: (0453) 2316; open 8am–noon and 1.30pm–6pm; admission charge*) has displays of traditional patterns and colours, and it also sells carpets.
*50km northeast of Sliven. Bus connections with Sliven.*

## Lovech (Ловеч)
One of the major beneficiaries of the Beautiful Bulgaria Project, the old town centre of Lovech is being carefully restored with over 160 buildings already completed in the Varosha Architectural Reserve, as the old town is known.

In the 19th century, Lovech was a hotbed of the revolutionary movement, being the central hub of Vasil Levski's national guerrilla cell network. It now plays host to the Revival and National Liberation Movement Museum, also known as the Vasil Levski Museum (*ul. Marin Pop Loukanov; open Tue–Sun 8am–noon and 2pm–6pm; admission charge*). Cobbled ul. Marin Pop Loukanov has other attractions, including an Ethnological Museum (*open summer daily 8am–noon and 2pm–5pm, winter Mon–Fri 8am–noon and 1pm–5pm; admission charge*) and the superb Byzantine Church of St Bogoroditsa (Church of the Holy Virgin).

You'll also want to see the Pokritiyat Most (covered bridge), with its rows of wooden shops. Designed by Ficheto (*see p72*) and originally built in 1872 (it was destroyed by fire in 1925 but was rebuilt), as it is unique in Bulgaria.

The large fortress atop the hill was the place where the treaty leading to the founding of the Second Bulgarian Empire was signed. The citadel now lies in evocative ruins.

*35km north of Troyan. Bus connections with Kazanluk, Sliven and Veliko Turnovo.*

## Madara (Мадара)

This humble modern village is famed for the 8th century bas-relief commonly called the Madara Horseman (Мадарски Конник) that is impressed into nearby cliffs. Carved in the 8th century AD to celebrate the military victories of Khan Tervel, who repelled an Arab invasion in the early years of the century and greatly expanded the territory of the First Bulgarian Empire, it features a mounted cavalryman, perhaps Tervel himself, spearing a lion.

Above the relief atop the cliffs, reached by a carved rock staircase, are the remains of the Madara Fortress, built in the 12th century to protect Bulgaria during the Second Empire (1185–1396).

*15km east of Shumen. Bus connections are poor but best from Shumen.*

The Madara Horseman

Oreshak plum brandy

### Oreshak (Орешак)

Most people visit tiny Oreshak, renowned for the production of plum brandy, for the Exhibition of Applied Arts and Traditional Crafts Complex (*Tel: (0670) 22 062; open Tue–Sun 9am–5pm; admission free*) to see and buy a comprehensive range of local handicrafts, including ceramics, embroidery, weaving and woodcarvings. The complex hosts one of Bulgaria's most famous fairs in late August each year. *7km west of Troyan. Bus connection with Troyan.*

### Shumen (Шумен)

The Shumen Fortress (*Open daily summer 7am–7pm, winter 8.30am–4pm; admission charge*), on the panorama overlooking the town and the valley, is Shumen's main tourist attraction. More than a simple citadel, its first walls were erected as early as the Iron Age (c. 8th century BC) and expanded under the Thracians and the Romans to house a whole community. Utilised by the Byzantines, it became a Bulgarian stronghold during the Second Empire, forming a pivotal cog in the country's protective shield. There's a model in the History Museum showing how the fort looked at its zenith. When Ottoman forces finally breached the walls the fortress' mighty defences were systematically neutralised, and later the stone was taken for other buildings in the town. Today the remains are an evocative place to explore, especially for lovers of castles and citadels. A maze of stout square buildings indicate where homes, shops and storerooms once stood. There's little explanation at the site, though the ticket office does have a rather old book on the history of the fort with a page in English.

On the range of hills across the valley and in clear sight of the fortress is the colossal Monument to the Founders of the Bulgarian State, erected in 1981 to commemorate the first Bulgarian Empire. From a distance it looks like a series of immense concrete blocks abandoned when a building project came to a halt. But close up, the series of titanic stone statues depicting the military heroes of the Bulgarian Empire, including a stylised Madara Horseman (*see previous page*), have an immense power and masculine beauty. In another section of the monument modern mosaics chart the influence of religion, including St Cyril surrounded by his alphabet.

Despite its rather grey mantle Shumen itself has a couple of attractions to visit. The Sherif Halili Pasha Mosque (known locally as the Tombul or Fat Mosque because of the shape of its huge dome) is said to be the largest mosque in the country still in use. Built in 1744, it is highly decorated. The History Museum (*bul. Slavyanski 17; tel: (054) 574 10; open Mon–Fri 9am–4.30pm; admission charge*) has one of the best collections in central Bulgaria, being particularly strong in Thracian artefacts and Roman finds from Veliki Preslav (*see p69*).
*15km north of Veliki Preslav. Bus connections with Burgas, Dobrich, Ruse and Veliko Turnovo.*

### Shipka (Шипка)

High in the Shipchenska Planina hills (part of the Stara Planina range), the 1300m high mountain pass at Shipka played an important role in the outcome of the Russian-Turkish War, when a force of Russian conscripts and Bulgarian volunteers repelled some 30,000 Turkish soldiers, a relief army for besieged forces further north at Pleven. Seven thousand defenders are thought to have died, considered heroes in both Bulgaria and Russia.

The major attractions here are both monuments to the lost. At the highest point along the route, atop Mt Stoletov, is the rather dour Freedom Monument erected in 1934 (*open daily dawn–dusk;*

Shumen fortress

admission free) offering fantastic panoramic views over the valleys below. At the base of the pass to the south, just outside Shipka village, is the glorious, colourful St Nikolai Church (*open daily 8.30am–5.30pm; admission charge*), built in 1902 in ornate Russian Orthodox style with onion domes smothered in gold. Inside lie the remains of many of the Russian fallen – a poignant final resting place so far away from their homes.

*18km north of Kazanluk. Bus connections with Kazanluk and Gabrovo.*

### Sliven (Сливен)

Set amidst the eastern Balkan Mountains' peaks, Sliven was the major hiding place of the Haidouks (*see pp78–9*), the Bulgarian rebels who waged a guerrilla war against the Turks throughout the 18th and 19th centuries, precipitating the Bulgarian Uprising. They survived for decades in the seemingly impenetrable Blue Rocks (*see p138*), now a national park where a chairlift whisks you with ease to the caves used as homes by the revolutionaries.

The town's History Museum (*ul. Tsar Osvoboditel 18; tel: (044) 22 494; open Mon–Fri 9am–noon and 2pm–5pm; admission charge*) predictably concentrates on the Haidouk story, displaying artefacts connected with the rebel action. It also displays a range of ancient finds excavated in the area but doesn't have captions in English.

The Hadzhi Dimitur House-Museum (*ul. Assenova 2; open Mon–Fri 9am–noon and 2pm–5pm; admission charge*) has a section dedicated to Hadzhi Dimitur, a leader of the rebel movement, but comprises several interesting 19th-century National Revival structures, including an old inn and ensemble of farm buildings.

*65km west of Stara Zagora. Bus connections with Karlovo, Plovdiv, Stara Zagora and Veliko Turnovo.*

### Stara Zagora (Стара Загора)

Although Stara Zagora lies on ancient foundations dating back to Thracian times, the city was razed by the Turks in 1877, an action that destroyed many magnificent Thracian, Roman and Byzantine remains. However, amongst the town's verdant avenues there are still some treasures to be found, including the Roman theatre on ul. Mitropolit, the forum on bul. Bishop Methodii Kousev, and mosaics on the floor of the main post office and on ul. General Stoletov.

Even more ancient are the 8,000-year-old houses at the Neolithic Dwellings Museum on Bereketska Mogila (*off bul. Dr Todor Stoyanovich; open Tue–Sat 9am–noon and 2pm–5pm; admission charge*), the largest and best preserved of such finds in Europe. The important discernable finds can be viewed in a separate gallery along with artefacts from other sites in the region.

*25km southwest of Kazanluk. Bus connections to Burgas, Kazanluk, Plovdiv, Sliven and Veliko Turnovo.*

### Troyan Monastery (Троянски Манастир)

Troyan is the third largest monastery in Bulgaria. Founded as late as the 16th century, it was badly damaged in several Turkish attacks during the 17th and 18th centuries and much was rebuilt during the expansion of the complex during the 1830s. It was at Troyan, always a hotbed of pro-Bulgarian activities, that Vasil Levski (*see p78*) finalised his new method of warfare – small, mobile guerrilla cells that proved a real thorn in the side of the Ottoman forces.

The monastery is renowned for its wood decoration, the highest quality hand carving by masters from Tryavna (*see pp68–9*). The revered Three-Handed Holy Virgin icon is its most precious possession, though this is only unveiled during the Assumption celebrations on 15th August. The church of the Holy Virgin, which houses the icon, was built in 1835 with murals by master artist Zahari Zograf though many are difficult to see because of soot deposits from the votive candles.

During the Bulgarian National Revival period the village of Troyan was renowned for its crafts. Today there seems little evidence of a living industry but it has a worthwhile Museum of Applied Art and Crafts (*pl. Vuzhrazhdane; tel: (0670) 22 063; open Tue–Sun 9am–5pm; admission charge*) with excellent displays of high-quality ceramics, weaving and woodcarving. *Monastery 10km east of Troyan village; open daily dawn–dusk. Admission free. Bus connection with Troyan village; connections from Troyan to Karlovo, Plovdiv and Veliko Turnovo.*

Troyan Monastery

Tryavna's stone bridge

## Tryavna (Трявна)

One of the architectural highlights of Bulgaria, Tryavna is one of a handful of living museums (others include Elena and Koprivshtitsa): a village seemingly left behind in the 19th century, a microcosm of all that is good in the Bulgarian National Revival (*see pp26–7*) style. The village was at the centre of the arts and crafts movement of the time, being particularly famed for its wood-carving. The artisans of Tryavna – graduates of the Tryavna School as it became known – were in high demand throughout the Balkans and Russia in the late 1800s. Today it is still a thriving artists' colony.

Tryavna is the least busy of the living museum villages and it's much easier to take in the detail as you stroll around. A good place to start is the main square in town, pl. Kapitan Dyado Nikola. Flanked by an ensemble of fine 19th-century buildings, it offers one of the best vistas in central Bulgaria. St Archangel Michael's Church sits on the square. Originally medieval (Second Bulgarian Empire), it was rebuilt in 1819 in the same style when the original edifice was set alight by the Turks. The interior is decorated with exceptional Tryavna school carvings. Staroto Shkolo (*pl. Kapitan Dyado Nikola 7; tel: (0677) 25 17; open daily, summer 9am–6pm, winter 9am–4.30pm; admission charge*), built in 1836, was the village school but has now been tastefully renovated to host an eclectic collection of ancient and modern art. The permanent collection is by contemporary artist Dimitar Kazakof and sculptor Zlatko Paunov, but they are juxtaposed by the displays of 19th-century objects used in the school.

From the square it's a short walk across the diminutive stone bridge to ul. Slaveikov, an exceptional cobbled street flanked by numerous noteworthy mansions. Visit the Museum of Woodcarving and Icon Painting in Daskalov House (*ul. Slaveikov 27. Tel:(0677) 2166; open daily summer 8am–noon and 1.30pm–5.30pm; winter 9am–4.30pm; admission charge*) for a collection of high-quality woodcarving from the Tryavna school. The house itself has some fine carved detail. At number 45 you'll find Kalinchev House (*Tel: (0677) 2166; open Mon–Fri 9am–4pm; admission charge, tickets at Daskalov House*), an 1830s mansion that has now been converted into a gallery displaying over 500 works by Bulgarian artists, including Troyan native Totyu Gabenski.

Other interesting buildings are the Museum of Icons (*ul. Breza 1; tel: (0677) 37 53; open 9am–4.30pm; admission charge*) and the 1805 Angel Kunchev House (*ul. Angel Kânchev; tel: (06770) 2398; open Tue–Sat summer 8am–6pm; winter 9am–4.30pm*) home of Bulgarian freedom fighter Angel Kunchev, which hosts a retrospective on his role in the independence movement.
*45km southwest of Veliko Turnovo. Bus connections with Gabrovo.*

## Veliki Preslav (Велики Преслав)
Founded in 821 by Khan Omurtag, Veliki Preslav (Great Preslav) became Bulgaria's original capital, when the First Empire was proclaimed under Tsar

Mosaic of Sts Cyril and Methodius in Veliki Preslav

Evocative remains of the old capital of Veliki Preslav

Simeon. At that time it was one of the most important cities in Europe, a hub of transport, trade and politics, but it suffered in the constant friction between Bulgaria and the Byzantines and was razed by the Turks when they rampaged across the country in 1388.

The extensive ruins of the old capital are fascinating for those who like their history unexcavated and un manicured. They extend over 5sq km – wear comfortable shoes – and you'll be able to explore the public baths, the workshop district and the remains of the old ramparts. The core of the city was the ancient walled citadel containing the old Royal Palace (*2km south of the modern town of Preslav; open 24 hours; admission free; guided tours in English, separate charge – contact the*

*Archaeological Museum*) and the remains of churches, storehouses and baths complexes. The Archaeological Museum (*adjacent to the ruins; tel: (0538) 2630; open daily summer 9am–6pm, winter 9am–5pm; admission charge*) displays a vast range of artefacts harvested from the site. Mundane items include pottery and tools; however, there are also treasures, including a stunning gold necklace and the old Royal seals.
*20km southwest of Shumen. Bus connections with Shumen.*

### Veliko Turnovo (Велико Търново)

'City of the Tsars,' Veliko Turnovo (also spelled Veliko Târnovo), meaning Great Turnovo, witnessed many of the pivotal moments in Bulgarian history. Capital of the country during the Second Empire (1185–1396), when it was second in importance only to Constantinople, it rose again during the National Revival period. In fact the Bulgarian state was proclaimed and the constitution written here following the departure of the Turks. However, it lost out to Sofia when a new capital of the post-Ottoman Bulgaria was decided.

The town's setting is spectacular. Surrounded by mountain peaks and cut by the deep sinuous gorge of the River Yantra, the dramatic Tsarevets and Trapezitsa hills bear down on the magnificent old town, which clings limpet-like to the sheer valley sides. The streets seemingly drape themselves one below the other, forming one of the most photographic vistas in Bulgaria.

The hills have been settled since the

Veliko Turnovo clings to the Tsarevets hillside

A street scene in old Veliko Turnovo

Neolithic period and Tsarevets forms a natural fortress which has been enhanced by man throughout the generations. First Thracians and then Romans fortified the hill but when the Byzantines arrived in the 5th century AD they made it a key citadel in their defences and it formed the heart of the Second Empire capital – then called Turnovgrad. Today, the Tsarevets fortress is one of Bulgaria's most impressive tourist attractions (*Tel: (063) 8841; open summer 8am–7pm, winter 9am–5pm; admission free*) Though large sections are little more than piles of rubble, the result of a final sacking by the Turks in 1393, the citadel once supported a population of thousands. The Patriarch's Complex sitting at the highest point on the hill has been restored and features a series of modern murals relating turning points in Bulgaria's history. Just below to the north is the Royal Palace and further north still the noblemen's quarters. To the south, on a precipitous crag, is Baldwin's tower, where the Byzantine emperor Baldwin was imprisoned before his execution in 1205.

An impressive evening light and sound show takes place at all times of year provided at least 300 leva has been collected in ticket fees (*for information tel: (063) 6828*). The show is easily visible from many quarters of the town, so it isn't limited to ticket holders.

From the fort you'll get dramatic views of the old town, which is one of the finest in Bulgaria. The streets are a

National Revival house, Veliko Turnovo

treasure trove of National Revival buildings, many the work of one architect, Kolyo Ficheto. As with many Bulgarian towns and villages, one simply has to stroll along the streets to soak in the architectural detail. Though many buildings are in the process of being renovated, many are also in desperate need of tender loving care. Most are not open to the public.

Two of the town's major museums relate to the founding of the Third Empire but with little explanation except in Cyrillic are of limited interest to non-Bulgarian speakers. The Museum of the National Renaissance and Constitutional Assembly (*ul. Ivan Vasov; open Wed–Mon 9am–6pm; admission charge*) is housed in the building where the first parliament of the free Bulgaria met to adopt the new constitution, and the Museum of Contemporary Bulgarian History (*ul. Tchtalischa; open Mon–Fri 8am–noon and 1pm–5pm; admission charge*) retraces the period of the Revolution with armaments, uniforms and old photographs of the time. Far more worthwhile is the Archaeological Museum (*ul. Ivan Vazov; tel: (063) 34946; open Tue–Sun 8am–noon and 1pm–6pm; admission charge*) which contains some excellent Second Empire artefacts from Tsarevets fortress and a large collection of Roman artefacts from nearby Nikopolis ad Istrum (*see p77*) and beyond.

The glorious setting of the State Art Gallery (*Assenovtsi Park; tel: (062) 38961; open Tue–Sun 10am–6pm; admission charge; guided tour in English, separate charge*), on the point of a sinuous curve in the river, is perhaps more inviting than the collection, which is limited to local artists. Overlooking the river in front of the gallery is the dramatic Monument of the Assens, erected to commemorate the founding of the Second Bulgarian Empire. There are excellent views over the old town from here.

Sarafkina House (*ul. Gurko 88; open Mon–Fri 9am–noon, 1pm–6pm; admission charge*) is worth a visit. Constructed in 1861 for a wealthy Turkish merchant, it houses a bijou but interesting Ethnographical Museum. The upper floor looks as if the family could still be living there, with genuine 19th-century interior design and furniture; there are even family photos on the walls.

Veliko Turnovo has numerous churches. The large cathedral (ul. Ivan Vazov) was designed by Ficheto in 1872, as was St Spas Church, which was abandoned after an earthquake in 1913. The Church of St Peter and St Paul (*ul. Mitropolska; open 9am–noon and 1pm–6pm; admission charge*) features some fine murals, the earliest from the 14th century. The Forty Martyrs Church (*ul. Mitropolska; open 9am–noon and 1pm–6pm; admission charge*) is the most interesting church in the town, however. Built in 1230 during the Second Empire, it became a royal mausoleum before being converted into a mosque during the Ottoman era. Today it houses a library of rare manuscripts. On the outskirts of town on the route to Arbanasi (*see pp54–5*) is the Church of St Dimitar (*ul. Patriarch Evtimii; open 9am–noon and 1pm–6pm; admission charge*). It was at the consecration of the church in 1185 that Tsars Assen and Petar declared the uprising that would eventually lead to the founding of the Second Bulgarian Empire.

*46km north of Gabrovo. Bus connections with Shumen, Gabrovo and Stara Zagora. Main line train station with connections to Pleven, Plovdiv, Ruse, Sofia, Stara Zagora and Varna. Tourist office ul. Hristo Botev; tel: (062) 21 48; open 9am–noon and 1pm–6pm.*

The State Art Gallery and Assens Monument

# Walk: Old Veliko Turnovo

Starting from the Tsarevets Fortress, this 5km walk takes about 3 hours.

### 1 Tsarevets Fortress

Start by exploring the fortress. This ruined citadel was the engine room of the Second Bulgarian Empire, when the royal family held court here. However, the most impressive remains today are the crenellated boundary walls and the renovated Patriarch's Complex with its distinctive belfry tower.

*Walk away from the fortress on ul. Ivan Vasov (ул Иван Вазов). After a couple of minutes on the left you'll find the major museum complexes of the town.*

### 2 Museums

The Museum of National Revival and Constituent Assembly is housed in the old neoclassical Town Hall. Next door is the Archaeological Museum, and behind this the Museum of Contemporary Bulgarian History, relating to the period of the uprising.

*From the museums walk straight ahead, keeping the Church of Konstantin and Elena (1872) on your right. This brings you to ul. Gurko (ул Гурко).*

### 3 ul. Gurko

Cobbled ul. Gurko is a typical 19th-century street with mansions with overhanging closed balconies. To the left you can look down the canyon to the river below and across to your ultimate destination, the State Art Gallery in Assenovtsi Park.

### 4 Sarafkina House

At 88 ul. Gurko you'll find Sarafkina House, constructed in 1861 for a banking family. The collection of

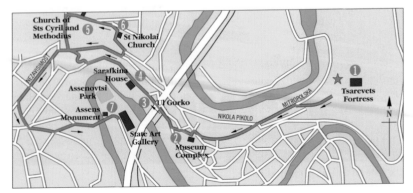

furniture and other pieces inside recreates its 19th-century splendour – a time when the town was emerging from years in the Ottoman doldrums.

*At the end of ul. Gurko climb up to the parallel street, the major arterial route through the town (this changes its name as it travels east to west through town but is unmistakeable because it's busy and lined with shops and cafés). Cross the street and take the flight of steps up into the Varosha district of town. The steps terminate at ul. Mednikarska (ул Медникарска). Walk straight across up ul. Slaveikov (ул Славеиков) then turn right at ul. Kiril & Metodii (ул Кирил и Методии).*

### 5  Sts Cyril and Methodius Church

Here on the corner you'll find the Church of Sts Cyril and Methodius, erected in 1861 with money donated by architect Ficheto. The church belfry is the highest point in the town.

*Turn right down ul. Kiril & Metodii and then right down ul. Tsipra (ул Ципра) to find St Nikolai Church on the left.*

### 6  St Nikolai Church

Erected in 1836, this church was Ficheto's apprentice piece.

*Walk down past the church then left and right to reach the main arterial route again. Turn right here and follow the road until you reach the junction with ul. Hristo Botev (ул Христо Ботев) (approximately 1km) where you'll take another left turn.*

*Walk past the tourist office on your left. When you reach the junction with ul. Stamboliiski (ул Стамболииски) turn left and walk down the street to*

Tsarevets Fortress

*Stambolov Most, the iron bridge over the Yantra gorge. Cross the bridge into Assenovtsi Park.*

### 7  Assenovtsi Park

At the northwestern tip of the promontory stands the monumental Monument to the Assens. This is a truly heroic creation, depicting a chariot being drawn by two horses in full flight, but the immense black obelisk adds an incongruous note. The State Art Gallery in the centre of the park is an impressive building with an immense collection of over 4,000 pieces. The museum has a café and terrace where you can sip a coffee while enjoying the breathtaking natural landscapes across the old town.

# Drive: Touring the Veliko Turnovo Countryside

Veliko Turnovo makes an excellent base from which to tour. Within a 30-minute radius of the town there is a varied range of attractions to keep the most fussy tourists happy, from ancient Roman remains and National Revival villages to Bulgarian wineries. This drive covers 65km and should take about 4 hours excluding stops.

*Leave Veliko Turnovo (Велико Търново) on the A4/E772 road east in the direction of Varna (Варна). After 10km take the left turn to the village of Lyaskovets (Лясковец).*

## 1 Lyaskovets

Surrounded by vines, this village has at its heart one of the best wine houses in Bulgaria. The Lyaskovets Winery and wine tours can be arranged but this must be done in advance (best through the tourist office in Veliko Turnovo). *Return to the main road and take a right turn back towards Veliko Turnovo. After*

*5km turn right off the road to Arbanasi (Арбанаси).*

## 2 Arbanasi

Arbanasi is one of the architectural highlights of central Bulgaria, a settlement founded in the 16th century that attracted the upper classes of Bulgarian society in the National Revival period. The village is large, so you'll need to stroll around, but there are excellent churches and mansions to explore, and also a selection of pretty restaurants where you can take lunch. *Return towards Veliko Turnovo on the Veliko Turnovo/Byala (Бяла) road (travel on out of the other side of Arbanasi, not the way you came in). This leads downhill towards Veliko Turnovo, offering excellent views of the Tsarevets Fortress and the river. Just before you enter the town, as the castle takes your attention, you'll see a small church behind a high wall on the right.*

## 3 Church of St Dimitar

This is the Church of St Dimitar, the oldest church in the town. It was here during the consecration of the church in 1185 that the Tsars declared an uprising against Byzantine domination that brought about the Second Bulgarian Empire.

*Continue on over the river and into Veliko Turnovo. At the top of the hill take a right turn in the direction of Ruse (Русе). After 8km look for a faded sign pointing left to Preobrazhenski Monastery (Преображенски Манастир). The access road (around 2.5km) is rough but passable.*

## 4 Preobrazhenski Monastery

This monastery was once one of the most powerful in the area, but today it's an evocative backwater set on a steep slope surrounded by woodland. Destroyed by the Turks, it was rebuilt at various times during the 19th century and doesn't seem to have been touched since then. The diminutive Church of the Transfiguration is decorated both inside and out with exceptional murals, including Zahari Zograf's *Circle of Life*

on the outside south wall.

*From the monastery continue toward Ruse (left at the junction of the main road from the monastery link road). After 10km look for a signpost to the village of Niykup/Nijkup (Нийкуп) (if you cross the river you have gone too far). Just outside the village you'll find the remains of the Roman settlement of Nikopolis ad Istrum.*

## 5 Nikopolis ad Istrum

Nikopolis ad Istrum was a Roman colonial town founded in 102AD and named by Emperor Trajan in commemoration of his victory over the Dacians. The best-preserved sections of the city, which was destroyed by barbarians in the 6th century, is the forum, but you can view excavated streets and the low walls of houses and shops.

*Return to the main road and turn right to make your way back to Veliko Turnovo.*

Preobrazhenski Monastery

# The Haidouks

'For a full twenty years did Chavdar, Stand at the head of his warriors,
A terrible Haidouk was Chavdar, For the chorbadjis and the Turks;
But for the poor and needy, A shield was Chavdar the chieftain!
Therefore his song was sung widely, By the forests of Strandjha Mountain,
By the grass upon Irin-Pirin, The honeyed pipe takes up the burden,
From Stamboul to Serbia's border'

Extract from *Haidouks Father and Son* by **HRISTO BOTEV**

Throughout the 15th to the 17th centuries the Bulgarian state was brought to a state of collapse by the weight of Ottoman rule. Deprived of the ability to form political institutions the Bulgarians found it difficult to organise any mass resistance. The Haidouks were the most successful and best known of the many locally based resistance fighters. Haidouks were fighters who left their homes to live in the mountains and woods, particularly in the Blue Rocks (see p66), sustaining the morale of the population but also the cause of many bloody reprisals as innocent villagers paid for Haidouk raids.

Over their long fight for freedom, the movement developed a sophisticated *modus operandi*, particularly under the guidance of Vasil Levski. This culminated in the April Uprising of 1876, when several regions rose up against the Turks. In itself the uprising was unsuccessful. Only the population of central Bulgaria rose with the rebels following a call to arms in Koprivshtitsa in 1876, and many were slaughtered to the last man in bloody battles – the worst at Batak. But it was the Ottoman reaction to this uprising that caused Russia to come to the defence of the Bulgarians – starting the Russian-Turkish War that ended Ottoman rule in Bulgaria.

## HAIDOUK LEADERS
### Vasil Levski (1837–1873)

Leader of the revolutionary forces, Levski (born Vasil Kunchev, he was given the nom de guerre 'Levski' or 'lion') trained as a monk but turned freedom fighter in 1862. His main success was in transforming the intellectual debate for freedom into an armed struggle by setting up numerous fighting or resistance cells (called *cheti*) throughout the country, operating free of any larger colonial influence. He often set up cells in monasteries – it is said that at Troyan (see pp66–7) he even tried to persuade the monks to join the rebel force. He was arrested in 1872 and executed in Sofia.

### Stefan Karadza (1840–1868)
Leader of a Levski *cheta*. He fought through the Balkan Mountains before being killed by the Turks. His *cheta* fought to the last man.

### Georgi Benkovski (1844–1876)
Successor to Levski, Benkovski hoped to introduce a system of government similar to those found in the revolutionary states of America and France.

### Hristo Botev (1848–1876)
One of the principal figures in the April Uprising, the poet Botev had just returned from exile in Romania in April 1876, travelling across the Danube on a seized Austrian packet boat. He was caught by the Turks and executed less than a month later.

### Georgi Sava Rakovski (1821–1867)
Early leader of the revolutionary movement, he organised the first formal armed groups to oppose the Ottoman Empire from a base in Belgrade. His dream of a Bulgarian army was never fulfilled in his lifetime.

### Lyuben Karavlov (c1835–1879)
Karavlov was the only revolutionary leader who lived to see an independent Bulgaria, dying in 1879.

Facing page: Vasil Levski statue, Dobrich
Below left: statue to Stefan Karadza
Below right: Shipka pass monument

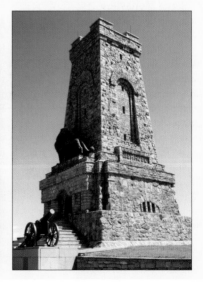

# Southwest Bulgaria

Three major mountain ranges shape the character of southwest Bulgaria. The Rila, Pirin and Rodopi ranges offer outstanding landscapes, from vertiginous peaks and high-altitude freshwater lakes to alpine meadow. Their most remote corners provide exceptional habitats for a range of creatures, particularly birds, and they also offer a year-round playground for human beings, with excellent summer hiking and winter sports opportunities.

Mountain stream near
Bansko

Heartland of the ancient Thracians, the region has seen the dusty footprints of many peoples cross its land throughout recorded time. There's much here for the history lover to enjoy, from ancient tombs to the most majestic of Bulgaria's monasteries.

## Bachkovo Monastery
## (Бачковоски Манастир)

Bachkovo was founded in 1083 by Georgian aristocrats Gregory and Abasi Bakuriani, who were commanders in the Byzantine army of Alexis I. It developed into a major religious complex during the Second Bulgarian Empire before being sacked by the Turks. The monastery recovered during the 17th century and today is the second richest and most influential in the country after Rila.

The approach road to the complex is flanked by perhaps 500m of souvenir stands, some selling rather inappropriate items of ladies' underwear, but these can be bypassed by parking just outside the monastery gates (parking charge).

Inside the walls, the large courtyard contains two churches. The 17th-century Church of the Assumption houses a miraculous silver icon of the Virgin, brought from Georgia in the 14th century, which is one of the most revered in Bulgaria, and a magnificent iconostasis. Unfortunately, the murals of the inner chamber have gathered a coating of soot from the votive candles and are difficult to see. The antechamber and outer gallery have brighter images.

The smaller 12th-century Archangel Church is decorated with exceptional 18th-century murals by Bulgarian Renaissance master artist Zahari Zograf. The St Nikolas Chapel (often closed) contains more murals by Zograf, including a worthy *Doomsday*, while the former refectory has an exceptional painted ceiling. The small museum on site contains a collection of icons, and you can also visit the 11th-century ossuary outside the complex on the far side of the car park.
*30km south of Plovdiv; open daily 6.30am–9pm. Admission free. Guided tours, with separate charge. Bus*

*connections from Asenovgrad, which can
in turn be reached from Plovdiv.*

### Bansko (Банско)

Bansko is on the brink of another
revival. Founded in the 15th century, in
the midst of the Pirin Mountains, the
town made money from the cultivation
of tobacco and from its traditional
crafts. It flourished during the National
Revival when the so-called Bansko
School of artists earned an international
reputation. However, since the year 2000
millions of euros have been invested in
winter sports facilities to ensure that the
town rivals Borovets, and this in turn
has been followed by several new 'alpine'
style hotels that should bring European
skiers in their droves.

Bansko has long been a popular
destination for Bulgarians. It makes
the perfect base for touring the wilds
of the Pirin National Park during the

Bachkovo Monastery

## Southwest Bulgaria

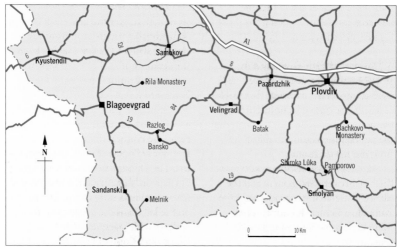

A street in Bansko

summer and the town itself has over 150 officially recognised cultural monuments. Many of the old mansions are now being converted into galleries and restaurants, so it's a great town for a relaxed stroll.

The clock tower in the grounds of the Sveta Troitsa (Holy Trinity) Church (*pl. Vazhrazhdane*) can be seen from most parts of the old town. The interior has carved wood decoration by the master Velyan Ognev and murals by the Bansko School. From here it's a short walk to all the major museums.

Velyanov House (*ul. Velyan Ognev 5; tel: (07443) 4181; open Mon–Fri 9am–noon and 2pm–5pm; admission charge*) is a 17th-century mansion owned by the carving master, worth seeing for its excellent murals and decorative wood ceilings.

Museum Nikola Vaptsarov (*pl. Nikola Vaptsarov 3; tel: (07433) 3038; open Mon–Fri 9am–noon and 2pm–5.30pm; admission charge*) displays an interesting collection of artefacts tracing Bansko's history and development. The main building of the museum was the family mansion of the Vaptsarov family. Vaptsarov himself was a poet but also a war hero and fervent anti-Fascist who was executed by the wartime Bulgarian regime. The annexe contains a quality arts and crafts gallery where many items are for sale.

The town also has an Icon Exhibition (*ul. Sandinski; tel: (07443) 4005; open Mon–Fri 9am–noon and 2pm–5pm; admission charge*) that displays a collection of mainly 19th-century examples.

At the top of the town the new gondola links Bansko to the winter ski runs or summer walking/hiking routes. It offers exceptional views of the mountains and the valley between the Pirin and Rila mountain ranges.
*60km southeast of Blagoevgrad.*
*Bus connections with Blagoevgrad, Plovdiv, and Sofia. Tourist information pl. Nikola Vaptsarov. Tel: (07443) 8374. Open daily summer 9am–8pm, winter 2pm–5pm.*

### Batak (Батак)

Bulgarians come to Batak to enjoy the summer activities of the nearby Batak Lake set amongst the western Rodopi Mountains, but the town is infamous in Bulgarian history for the massacre of over 5,000 townspeople by the Turks during the uprising of 1876. It was this incident above all others that caused

Russia to declare war on the Ottoman Empire, a bitter and bloody conflict that brought about the end of Turkish rule in Bulgaria.

The Church of Sveta Nedelya still bears witness to the final fate of over 2,000 townsfolk taking refuge here during the Battle of Batak. Bullet holes riddle the walls and a few damaged skulls rest in an open tomb. The town's History Museum also has some moving displays on the atrocity.
*80km southwest of Plovdiv. Bus connection with Plovdiv.*

## Blagoevgrad (Благоевград)

One of the centres of modern Bulgarian learning and culture, Blagoevgrad, named in 1950 in honour of Dimitar Blagoev, one of the founders of Bulgarian communism, boasts two universities and over 20,000 students. Though the town has little in the way of historical attractions it has a young and vital atmosphere with some excellent bars and cheap eateries.

The History Museum (*ul. Rila 1; tel: (073) 85370; open Mon–Fri 9am–noon and 1pm–6pm; admission charge*) is worth a visit for the vast collection of artefacts from the Neolithic period to the early 20th century, though there are no captions in English. The highlight is the icons section.
*100km south of Sofia. Bus connections with Bansko and Sofia. Town website www.blgmun.com. Tourist information: Pirin Tourist Forum, Ul. Komitrov 8; tel: (073) 36795; fax: (073) 35458, website www.pirin-tourism.bg.
Open Mon–Fri 8.30am–6.30pm, Sat summer only 10am–4pm)*

Tobacco crops drying at Blagoevgrad

## Borovets (Боровец)

In the heart of the Rila Mountains, Borovets is a major international winter resort (*see pp100–101*) and summer hiking base. The town itself is tiny, being little more than a collection of modern hotels and associated cafés, restaurants, souvenir stalls and nightclubs, but it offers a superb setting, surrounded by peaks swathed in verdant pine forests.

*75km southeast of Sofia. Bus connections with Samokov. Tourist information at the Rila Hotel complex. Tel: (07128) 2441. Open Mon–Fri 9am–5pm.*

## Melnik (Мелник)

Capital of Bulgarian wine (*see pp170–71*), Melnik sits in the very far southwestern corner of the country,

Borovets caters for tourism in the summer as well as in its main winter season

close to the Greek border. Set in a sheltered sandy valley, its local soils and Mediterranean climate are excellent for vines.

During the 13th century the region became the personal fiefdom of Alexei Slav. He reigned for only a short time but the remnants of several fortresses and monasteries are a legacy of his rule. The town was one of the wealthiest in the country in the late 19th century by virtue of the wine and tobacco trade but it remained under Ottoman control until 1912, losing markets in the newly independent Bulgaria. Its population has dwindled to a fraction of its peak after a fire destroyed much of the town during the Balkan War (1912–13). It is officially Bulgaria's smallest town, with less than 300 inhabitants, but it possesses a number of well-renovated National Revival mansions and plenty of evocative ruins. Visitors also come to see the strange natural rock formations in the nearby cliffs – erosion has produced surreal shapes such as chimneys and columns.

It's best to park the car at the bottom of the village by the main road, as there are no tarmac roads to the houses. From the main thoroughfare beside the stream narrow alleyways lead up the hillsides to the main attractions.

The wine theme starts at Kordopoulov Kashta (House) (*Tel: 07437) 265; open when the guardian is on duty – no set hours; admission charge*). Built in 1754 for a wealthy wine merchant, it is said to be one of the largest National Revival buildings in the country, with a labyrinth of hand-hewn cellar/caves for wine storage.

Now village-sized, Melnik was once a thriving commercial town

You can taste and buy the robust Melnik wines at Mitko Manolev Wineries. There are tables set out in a cool cave where the wine is stored or out on the small terrace that offers excellent views across the rooftops. There are several wine bars on the main street to enjoy the odd glass or two. Damianitza Winery (*www.melnikwine.bg*) offers tasting and wine tours but it's best to book ahead.

Visit the tiny History Museum (*Tel: (07437) 229; open daily 9am–noon and 1pm–5pm; admission charge*) for some fascinating photographs of Melnik as a lively metropolis 100 years ago. It also features a collection of local handicrafts.

Dominating the heights above the town is the Fortress of Alexei Slav, built in the 13th century. Bolyarskata Kashta, the home of the Slav family (not to be confused with the race of people called Slavs), was built in the 10th century and there are good views over the village from here, but both structures now lie in ruins.

*80km south of Blagoevgrad. Bus connections with Blagoevgrad and Sandinski.*

Traditional farming at Melnik

## Pamporovo (Пампорово)

Pamporovo, Bulgaria's most up-market ski resort (*see pp100–101*), sits in the heart of the Rodopi Mountains. In the last few years it has also been opening up as a summer destination with beautiful surroundings of spruce and pine forest. It's also one of the most expensive places to stay outside the capital.

Pamporovo takes its name from the mule trains (*pampor*) that used to run through the high pass from Smolyan during the Ottoman era. Its first accommodation was opened in 1933.

*16km north of Smolyan. Bus connections with Chepelare, Plovdiv and Smolyan. Tourist office near the Hotel Perelik. Tel: (03021) 236; www.pamporovo.net.*

## Pazardzhik (Пазарджик)

Established by the Turks after the Crimean War, Pazardzhik developed quickly into one of the most important commercial towns in the eastern Ottoman Empire. It remained a mainly Muslim settlement until the 1960s but lost all influence during the Third Bulgarian Empire and communist rule. Today, perhaps because of its association with hated Turkish rule, the town has become inextricably linked throughout Bulgaria with thievery and scams, a reputation that the evidence shows is undeserved.

Renowned Bulgarian artist Stanislav Dospevski (1826-1876) was a native of the town. The house where he was born (*bul. Maria Luisa 54; tel: (034) 250 30; open Mon–Fri 9am–noon and*

2pm–5.30pm; admission charge) is now dedicated to the artist, preserving his personal effects and displaying several of his pieces. More are on display in the Stanislav Dospevski Gallery (*pl. Konstantin Velichkov 15; tel: (034) 257 21; open Mon–Fri 9am–noon and 2pm–5.30pm; admission charge*) which offers a more comprehensive collection of his art and sculpture.

The two main religions also have fine edifices. The Kurshum Dzhamiya (mosque), built in 1667, is the largest in Bulgaria after Plovdiv's, while the Sveta Bogoroditsa Cathedral, in archetypal National Renaissance style, was erected to mark the foundation of the Third Bulgarian Empire. Its wooden iconostasis carved by the Debur School is unique in Bulgaria.

*120km east of Sofia. Train connections with Sofia and Plovdiv. Bus connections with Batak, Sofia and Plovdiv.*

### Plovdiv (Пловдив)

Plovdiv is Bulgaria's second largest city. The site, set on several low hills on the banks of the Maritza River, has been settled for millennia as it sits at the junction of two ancient trade routes – the motorways of their day. Plovdiv has thrived through every era of the country's long and complicated history and it is here of all places that different strands of time can be seen lying cheek by jowl. The city's many treasures deserve at least a couple of days to explore fully.

The antecedents of today's Plovdiv can be traced back to the Thracians.

Plovdiv sits in a superb hilly location

Plovdiv was already an ancient settlement when these Roman columns were first erected

They fortified the site as early as 5000BC. Philip II of Macedonia captured the Thracian town, known as Eumolpias, in 341BC. He renamed the city Philipopolis and greatly expanded the complex. Under Roman rule the town was named Trimontium and then renamed again during the First Bulgarian Empire. Plovdiv was badly damaged during the Ottoman invasion but was rebuilt by the Turks, who called it Philibe. It flourished again following independence, when it developed a unique form of architecture incorporating elements of baroque and National Revival design now seen both restored and in ruins in the magnificent old town.

The oldest extant ruins are the remains of Thracian Eumolpias that perch atop 200m high Nebet Tepe (Nebet Hill). Though there's little to see apart from remnants of what were once immense walls, the hill offers good views across the rest of the city.

The Romans left a few traces (though sadly many were destroyed in later conflicts). The most bizarre are the excavated remains of a Roman stadium (the curved seats of the eastern end) that lie in an open city underpass with the concrete pillars of modern buildings resting on their marble terraces. The most impressive Roman site is without doubt the Amphitheatre (*ul. Hemus/ul. Tsar Ivailo; open daily 9am–5pm; admission charge*) built during the reign of Emperor Trajan in the 2nd century AD. The structure lay underground until 30 years ago, probably buried as the result of an earthquake, and was only rediscovered by accident. It has since been rather over-restored and now plays host to opera and folk events during the summer. The most disappointing remains have to be the scant sections of the forum (though the rest must lie underneath the main post office).

Religious buildings illustrate the period of Ottoman rule. Many Byzantine churches were destroyed in the Turkish invasion and so the city's churches are normally 16th- or 17th-century buildings resting on earlier foundations. Sts Konstantin and Elena (*ul. Saborna 24*) is the oldest, tracing its history back to the 4th century, though the current church dates from the 1830s. The highlights are the gilded iconostasis and collection of icons. The Sveti

Nedelya Church (*ul. Slaveikov 40*) was erected in 1578 and should be visited for the walnut iconostasis installed in the 17th century. Here, too, the icons are impressive.

The Dzhumaya Mosque dominates the square of the same name. Erected in the 15th century it's still in use, though many of the almost fifty others built during Ottoman rule have fallen into disrepair. It's worth visiting the smaller Imaret Mosque (*ul. Han Krubat*) for its 15th-century lavish interior decoration.

The 19th-century district of Plovdiv is exceptional: a maze of cobbled lanes flanked with fine mansions characterised by brightly coloured façades and overhanging upper floors supported by columns, a style only found here. Though you may be happy simply to take in the vistas, several buildings are worth a special mention and a visit.

Hindlian House was built for wealthy Plovdiv merchant Stefan Hindlian in 1835. The fabric of the house has been thoroughly restored and is furnished with excellent period pieces. Balabanov House (*ul. Stoilov 57; tel: (032) 627 082; open daily 9am–12.30pm and 1pm–5.30pm; admission charge*) is another merchant's house. It was completely rebuilt from the original plans during the 1980s, and so offers an ideal opportunity to view the style and methods of the architecture as they would have appeared when newly built. The ground floor now contains an art gallery but the upper floors display furniture of the Balabanov family. Danov House (*ul. Slaveikov 5; tel: (032) 266 804; open Mon–Sat 9am–12.20pm*

*and 2pm–4.30pm; admission charge*) pays homage to Hristo Danov, a famed Bulgarian writer, along with other native authors. Displays include some of the earliest newspapers printed in Bulgaria. For a slightly different experience, head to the Old Hippocrates Pharmacy (*ul. Saborna 1. Open Mon–Fri 9am–5pm; admission charge*). This chemist's shop is unchanged since the late 19th century, its shelves lined with bottles of unguents and potions.

Plovdiv's major museums provide a general overview of the long history of the town. The Archaeological Museum (*pl. Saedirenie 1; tel: (032) 269 933; open Mon–Fri 9am–noon and 1pm–5pm; admission charge*) displays only a

Gateway through Plovdiv's walls

fraction of its vast inventory but this includes items dating from the Neolithic period to the medieval era, including Thracian, Roman and Byzantine artefacts. By contrast, the Ethnographic Museum (*ul. Dr Chomakov 2; tel: (032) 62 56 54; open daily summer 9am–noon and 2pm–5.30pm, winter 9am–noon and 2pm–5pm; admission charge*) offers a wide range of objects from furniture and jewellery to traditional handicrafts housed in an exceptional National Revival house built in 1847. There are also good displays of the old trades that kept Plovdiv's economy buoyant – tobacco, wine and handicrafts such as pottery and weaving.

*140km east of Sofia. Train connections with Burgas, Karlovo, Sofia and Stara Zagora. Bus connections with Karlovo, Sofia and Stara Zagora.*

## Rila Monastery (Рилски Манастир)

It is ironic that a monastery founded by a hermit should today be Bulgaria's most visited and photographed attraction, but Rila, now a UNESCO World Heritage Site, is perhaps a microcosm of everything that Bulgaria offers to visitors – a spectacular natural setting, exquisite traditional architecture and extravagant religious art.

Founded by Ivan Rilski, also known as John of Rila, in 927, the original Rila complex sat a little way to the northwest but was moved to its present location in 1335, after which it consolidated its position as the most influential monastery in southwestern Bulgaria. It received regular and munificent gifts from the Bulgarian royal family and became an important centre of learning

and culture, drawing the finest scholars and artists of each generation. It also negotiated diplomatic accords with other powerful monasteries in Greece and Russia.

During the long years of Ottoman rule, Rila was a strong defender of Bulgarian national identity, keeping the Orthodox faith alive and preserving the nation's culture. Its library has over 16,000 editions, many rare handwritten parchments. The monastery suffered serious damage from insurgents in the early 15th century and a fire in 1833. Much of the complex dates from after 1833, when new donations from across Bulgaria allowed massive investment using the most renowned artisans of their day.

The monastery lies at the heart of the mountains that also bear John of Rila's name. Several precipitous peaks are so close that they seem to peer into the complex over the top of the walls, adding to the wonderful views. The monastery is built within an irregular quadrangle of fortified walls featuring two entrance gates (the Dupnitza to the west and the Samokov to the east).

At the centre of the interior space sits the magnificent Church of the Nativity, one of the religious masterpieces of the National Revival. Built between 1834 and 1837 in contrasting rows of cream and red tile and stone, it is blanketed in rich murals from the 1840s depicting Old Testament scenes painted by master Zahari Zograf (though its certain he had the help of other artists). These are still fairly bright despite the smoke from votive candles. The church also features perhaps the best iconostasis in Bulgaria, begun by Telador and six assistants in 1839. Featuring a riot of intricately carved flowers, animals and human figures framed by columns of vines it also depicts several biblical scenes. The exterior gallery of the church is also replete with murals whose colours are richer than those of the interior, so it's much easier to take in the detail.

The monastery's museum houses a notable number of artefacts, among them precious icons and other liturgical objects. The museum also proudly displays Rila's charter, signed in 1378 after it moved to its present site. However, pride of place is given to the renowned Rila Cross or Raphael's Cross (*see box*).

The rest of the monastery complex sits around the church and the 25m high

Hrelyu Tower, the only surviving element of the 1335 building, with a small ornate chapel, the Preobrazhenski or Transfiguration Chapel on the upper floor.

Designed in high Revival style, the abbot's quarters, cells for over 300 monks, the high-ceilinged kitchen,

### The Rila Cross

The most famous of Rila's artefacts is this wooden cross, also called Raphael's Cross. Created from one piece of wood 80cm by 43cm, it is carved with 104 miniature scenes from the Bible featuring more than 650 figures – many no bigger than a grain of rice. Raphael – a monk at the monastery – carved the scenes using a pin as his only tool. As he worked on the piece his eyesight suffered and after 12 years he became blind, so much was he willing to suffer to finish the piece.

Rila Monastery, Bulgaria's top tourist attraction

the bakery and the storerooms are all built into the outer walls, which rise to four storeys with a double-arcaded portico all around the complex and wooden balustrades on the upper balconies, which offer panoramic views of the surrounding Rila Mountains. The wooden balconies that punctuate the upper floors are the epitome of Revival style, with ornate wooden carving and gaily painted cornice detail. Four small chapels built in the shape of the Dome of the Cross have also been incorporated into the walls. Each features fine woodcarving and exceptional murals.

There are several other churches in the surrounding hills, all belonging to Rila and reached by footpath. One hour's walk (indicated along a path) from the monastery is the tomb of founder St John or Ivan Rilski in a cave in the forest (*see walk on pp98–9*). The bones were interred here some 600 years after the saint's death following their transference to Sofia and Veliko Turnovo. On the way you'll pass St Luke's Hermitage, whose church dates from 1799.

*110km south of Sofia. Open 8.30am–8pm. Museum 8.30am–4.30pm. Monastery: admission free. Museum: admission charge. Guided tours in English, separate charge. Bus connections with Rila village, from where there are connections to Blagoevgrad.*

## Rozhen Monastery (Роженски Манастир)

One of the least visited monasteries, Rozhen, officially called the Nativity of the Virgin Mary Monastery, is also the

An icon in Rozhen Monastery

best of the major monastery complexes in Bulgaria to capture the atmosphere of spiritual peace and contemplation. The simplicity of its internal décor is in total contrast to Rila and hints at a more simple life of monastic devotion. Originally founded in 1217, Rozhen was razed by the Turks in the 16th century, and much of what you see today dates from after 1730.

The main church in the monastery, however, dates from 1600 and contains some excellent decoration, including – unusually – some fine, though small, stained-glass windows as well as the more usual murals. The complex refectory is also highly decorated but the rest of the complex features rustic wooden staircases, balconies and balustrades and plain lime-washed walls.

The small church close to the entrance to the monastery is that of Sts Cyril and Methodius and shelters the tomb of Yane Sandanski (1872–1915), a noted Macedonian freedom fighter. *7km northeast of Melnik. Open dawn–dusk. Admission free but donations welcomed. Bus connections from Melnik and Sandanski to Rozhen village.*

## Samokov (Самоков)

The first seeds of socialist rule were planted here with the infamous declaration of a commune in 1912 but this experiment in social planning only lasted for two years. Little evidence remains in the town today of that event. Samokov was founded on iron mining and smelting – the town name derives from the Bulgarian word for forge – but was most famed before the commune for its school of icon painting in the 1800s which produced such luminaries as Zahari Zograf.

The History Museum (*Tel: (0722) 26 772; open Mon–Fri 8am–noon and 1pm–5pm; admission charge*) brings all these diverse strands together with its displays charting the development of iron smelting and old photographs. Other buildings worth visiting are the Dzhamiya Bairakli Mosque (*Main square; open Fri–Tue 8am–noon and 1pm–5pm; admission charge; tours in English separate charge*), a magnificent National Revival-style edifice constructed in 1840 as the Ottoman grip on power began to falter, the Convent of Sveta Bogoroditsa (*ul. Boris Hadjsotirov 77; open daily 6am–8pm;*

*admission free*), with its late 17th-century frescoes, and the Church of the Assumption, which possesses an iconostasis of the Samokov School. *60km southeast of Sofia. Bus connections with Borovets, Maliovitsa, Plovdiv and Sofia.*

### I Know the Score!

The small village of Rupite, close to Petrich on the Greek border, was the home of famed Bulgarian clairvoyant Baba Vanga (died 1996), a noted communist. It was her ability to predict the results of football matches that brought her to national attention. Many Bulgarians profited at the bookmakers by following her tips. Because of her influence, Rupite is now the centre of the Bulgarian New Age movement.

Dzhamiya Bairakli Mosque, Samokov

Rural scene near Shiroka Lûka

## Sandanski (Сандански)

Birthplace of the legendary Roman slave leader Spartacus, Sandanski sits close to the Greek border. Until 1949, the town was named Melnik but became Sandanski in honour of Macedonian freedom fighter Yane Sandanski. It is known for its thermal springs and balneo-therapeutic clinics but also offers an alternative base for hiking in the Pirin Mountains.

*65km south of Blagoevgrad. Train connections with Blagoevgrad and Sofia. Bus connections with Blagoevgrad, Melnik, Rozhen and Samokov.*

## Shiroka Lûka (Широка Дька)

An exceptionally picturesque settlement incorporating fine National Revival mansions and three Roman bridges, Shiroka Lûka is a protected architectural treasure but is less busy than Koprivshtitsa (*see p61*), allowing you more time to contemplate the architecture. The town is famed for its traditional Bulgarian music and holds one of the most colourful traditional festivals, the *kukeri*, in early March each year, when masked and costumed locals prowl the streets eager to exorcise any lurking demons in order to ensure a good harvest in the coming summer.

*15km west of Pamporovo. Bus connection with Smolyan.*

## Smolyan (Смолян)

Though not a particularly picturesque place in itself, Smolyan, an amalgam of four once independent villages, makes a good base for exploring the central Rodopi Mountains. The town does, however, boast a worthy Historical Museum (*pl. Bulgaria 3; tel: (0301) 62 727; open Tue–Sun 9am–noon and 1pm–5pm; admission charge*) tracing a chronological journey through Bulgaria's long past. There's a collection of excellent funerary artefacts from throughout the Thracian period, a huge section on the Bulgarian National Revival and displays of Bulgarian handicrafts, all with useful English captions.

Art lovers will enjoy the Smolyan Gallery (*Cultural Complex, pl. Bulgaria; tel: (0301) 23 969; open Tue–Sun 9am–noon and 1.30pm–5pm; admission charge*), which displays over 400 paintings by Bulgarian artists dating from the 19th century to the present day.

*20km south of Pamporovo. Bus connections with Pamporovo, Plovdiv and Shiroka Lûka. Tourist office: ul. Bulgar 5. Tel: (0301) 62 530, www.rodopi–bg.com. Open daily 9am–noon and 12.30pm–5pm.*

The Rodopi Mountains offer walks through unspoilt scenery

# Walk: Plovdiv History

With some of the finest examples of Bulgarian National Revival Architecture in Bulgaria, the old district of Plovdiv is a picturesque place to wander, with mansions, museums, small shops and pretty cafés to enjoy at every turn. This 3km walk will take you from the modern centre to the oldest existing remains of the city, while allowing you to really soak in the street atmosphere. Wear comfortable shoes as the traditional cobbles of the 19th-century district are uneven and can be slippery in wet weather.

*Allow 4 hours with visits.*

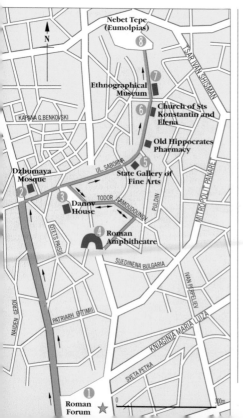

*Start at pl. Tsentralen (Площад Центяален), the rather dowdy heart of the modern city, marked by the Trimontium Princess Hotel and a monstrosity of a post office building.*

## 1 Roman Forum

Just behind (to the north of) the post office are the excavated remains of the Roman forum, looking rather lost amongst the mass of concrete.
*From the square, walk north up ul. Knyaz Alexander Battenberg (Кнйаз Алежандер Баттенберг), the main shopping street of Plovdiv, with a few international high-street brand names you might recognise.*

## 2 Mosque Square

At the top of Battenberg you'll spot the minaret of the Dzhumaya Mosque, one of the most recognisable landmarks in the city. The small square beside the mosque is filled with artists' stalls; the owners work on new pieces as they wait for customers to peruse their displays.

The square is dominated by a column supporting a stylised modern statue of a Roman Caesar and one look below ground level into the underpass reveals why – this is also the site of the Roman stadium, parts of which now poke out from underneath later buildings.

*From the mosque square take ul. Saborna (Саборна) (right and behind the mosque from the direction you entered), from where you'll begin to climb into the 19th-century district. Saborna is renowned for its antique shops, though the whole district has shops selling anything from genuine antiques to old knick-knacks.*

### 3 Danov House

Danov House sits on the right here in a shady garden. The mansion was owned by celebrated writer and publisher Hristo Danov and its displays showcase the lives of several other Bulgarian authors.

*Take the first right beyond Danov House, in front of the Church of the Holy Virgin, then second right (behind the church) along ul. Samokov (Самоков) and right again to ul. Tsar Ivailo (Цар Ивайло) to find the Roman Amphitheatre.*

### 4 Roman Amphitheatre

Built in the 2nd century AD and only rediscovered in 1972 following a landslide in the city, today the amphitheatre has been renovated (some would say overly so) and plays host to open-air performances in the summer.

*From the amphitheatre retrace your steps back to Saborna and continue uphill.*

### 5 Gallery of Fine Arts

The neoclassical State Gallery of Fine Arts appears on the right. This displays a fine collection of Bulgarian art from the 17th to the 20th centuries. Beyond this is the Old Hippocrates Pharmacy. If it isn't open at least you can look through the windows.

*Continue up Saborna and you'll find the Church of Sts Konstantin and Elena at the brow of the hill.*

### 6 Church of Sts Konstantin and Elena

This is the longest-standing church in the city, having been founded in 337 by the Roman Emperor Constantine, though the extravagant murals date from the 1830s when the church was last rebuilt.

*It is at this point that the best of Plovdiv reveals itself. Narrow cobbled streets run off left and right tempting you to leave the main route – each with its own fine buildings worthy of attention. Our route continues uphill along ul. Dr Chumakov (ул Чумаков).*

### 7 Ethnographic Museum

On the southeast corner of Chumakov, behind high walls, is the Ethnographic Museum, with a series of excellent displays on Bulgarian traditional lifestyles and customs.

*On past the museum and Chumakov peters out as you walk past a series of endearing but unrenovated National Revival mansions, some still being used as family homes, to reach the summit of Nebet Tepe.*

### 8 Nebet Tepe

Atop the hill are the remains of the old Thracian settlement of Eumolpias, where you'll benefit from wonderful vistas over the whole city.

# Walk: Kiril Meadows

A host of reasonably signposted footpaths lead out into the hills and mountains surrounding Rila Monastery, where you can forget the crowds and enjoy the dense forests. However, most involve steep climbs and require sturdy footwear. This walk for the most part follows the road that leads beyond Rila to a mountain basin. The route requires only comfortable footwear rather than specialist hiking boots and the inclines are gradual, so it's perfect for people of limited fitness. It will reward you with breathtaking mountain views and, aside from passing vehicles, all you'll hear is the sound of the nearby flowing stream and constant birdsong.

*There and back is 13.5km – allow 5 hours.*

*Leave your vehicle in the car park at the monastery and explore the incredible murals in the Church of the Nativity and other parts of the complex before departing through Samokov Gate (the eastern gate), where you'll see the road in front between cafés and a large souvenir shop.*

*The beginning section of the walk is almost flat and there are several cafés on the roadside. You'll hear the stream on*

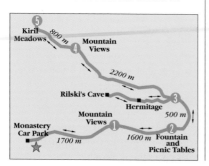

*your right and you'll walk past the Tsarev Hotel also on your right. Tightly packed pine trees hug the roadside, leaving you little chance to view the wider vista. You'll walk past a right junction before passing the Zodiac Hotel (also on your right) after 1300m.*

**1** At 1.7km the trees recede from the roadside, offering you the first opportunity to view the Rila Mountain peaks to your left and right before the forest encroaches again.

**2** After 3.3km you'll come to a water fountain and some picnic tables on the right. If you didn't bring bottled water with you on the trip the pure spring water here is perfectly safe to drink.

*A couple of hundred metres beyond the fountain the road swings left and begins to climb more steeply (though it is still a gradual rather than sudden climb).*

**3** Around this first bend (3.8km from the start of the walk) is a footpath leading to the St Luke's Hermitage and the tomb of monastery founder Ivan Rilski. Look for the tiny white signpost with the phrase На св. иван Рилски Гробът and a painted image of St Ivan with Кьм Гробъа above it.

This part of the walk (around 1 hour return) is over ground not tarmac. It leads first to the Hermitage (1843) containing two churches, the Church of St Luke (1799) with a monumental 35-scene Last Judgement mural, and the Church of the Shroud of the Virgin (1805) built by Mihail, a renowned mason from nearby Rila village. The path then carries on to the cave where Rilski lived, having taken a vow to end his days as a hermit. The bones of the saint are now interred here.

*Return to the road and continue the*

St Ivan's signpost

*gradual climb to your journey's end (by turning left).*

**4** After 6km the forest recedes once again to reveal an impressive rocky crest high above you to the left.

**5** At 6.8km you reach your destination, a low-lying bowl of grassland and pine forest surrounded on all sides by the Rila Mountains. The views are stupendous and you can picnic under the trees or take advantage of the handful of cafés on site. Further footpaths lead off to higher altitudes, including one that forms part of the E4 Euro-footpath linking the Pyrenees, Alps, Rila and Peloponnese ranges. *From here it's all downhill back to the monastery!*

Гробът на Св. Иван Рилски

Signpost to St Luke's Hermitage and Rilski's tomb

# Skiing in Bulgaria

Classed as one of Europe's best-value winter sport destinations, Bulgaria has an excellent snow record and offers an excellent choice for the beginner and intermediate skier, though it may not please the 'on-the-edge' thrill seeker searching for the ultimate off-piste experience. So which area do you choose that meets your needs?

## Mount Vitosha

This is just a stone's throw from Sofia, so you could combine a winter cultural visit to the capital with some time on the piste. Thirty kilometres of runs range from green to black, based around Aleko station, but there are disadvantages. Weekends and holidays are impossibly overcrowded with locals out to enjoy the snow. Also because most skiers bring their own equipment it's difficult to hire. The infrastructure is also rather old and pistes are not well maintained.

## The Rila Mountains

Borovets is the oldest resort in Bulgaria, established in 1896: a compact centre with three separate satellite settlements (a minibus operates between hotels and the slopes) set in verdant pine forest. The resort has one gondola, 2 chairlifts and 8 surface lifts to cover 50km of pistes, the longest of which is 6km. If you are flying in on a package it's a relatively short transfer from Sofia airport (70km).

Maliovitsa is a tiny resort with a couple of hotels and one draglift to serve the few runs, but it's cheaper than Borovets and perfectly adequate for an afternoon of fun.

## The Pirin Mountains

Bansko has the best snow record of any Bulgarian resort (often enough snow to ski until the end of May) and was a secret the Bulgarians kept to themselves, but it's on the brink of a new era with

the erection of a state-of-the-art gondola linking the village centre to the slopes (12km away by road). Around the gondola, several new hotels have sprung up, so Bansko is preparing to take its slice of the skiing market. The main disadvantage is a long transfer from the airport at Sofia (150km) and an as yet untried infrastructure – ski hire, instruction, etc.

## The Rodopi Mountains

Pamporovo is a modern purpose-built resort with a total of 18km of well-maintained pistes (25 runs and 18 lifts, 13 of which are drag lifts) aimed at beginners, intermediates and especially families. The ski-school here is well established, with multilingual instruction and kids-only lessons. The transfer from Sofia is a long one but most charter flights arrive at Plovdiv only 90km to the north. One disadvantage is that it is

rather spread out and lacking in charm, the opposite of Borovets.

Chepelare (two chair lifts only) is a smaller satellite of Pamporovo but its two main runs are considered to be the best in Bulgaria, and the blue run through the trees is exceptionally pretty.

To make the most of your skiing budget you may find it cheaper to book a package from home rather than travel independently. Hotels and ski hire shops aren't as geared up for walk-in clients as other European destinations and can charge an extortionate 'rack rate' supplement. You'll also be guaranteed to get decent hire equipment with your package. Look for deals with the major winter snow travel companies.

## Ski Run Grading

Ski runs in Europe are graded by colour: Greens are the easiest, Blues are slightly more difficult, Reds are more challenging and Blacks are for experts only.

Facing page:
Bulgarian resorts can be relied on for snow, often until quite late in the season
This page: Borovets ski banner

# The Black Sea Coast

Bulgaria's Black Sea coast is its tourism Mecca. It plays host to masses of visitors from Western Europe together with a loyal contingent from Russia. The first tourists arrived in the late 19th century to take the mineral waters found at sources close to Varna, but today it's the fantastic beaches and warm summer weather that are the major draws. Most holidaymakers stay in one of the three huge modern man-made resorts built since the 1960s but it's important to break out of these anonymous pleasure domes to enjoy the numerous historical and natural attractions that the coast has to offer.

Picturesque Balchik

## Albena (Албена)

Self-styled 'sports capital' of the Black Sea, the modern resort of Albena is set on a spectacular 4km long beach (*see p122*) and offers the most comprehensive range of summer holiday activities in Bulgaria. For this reason it's also the most international of resorts, with the most up-to-date and comprehensive infrastructure. Established in 1969 on the site of several mineral springs, the town is named after the heroine of one of Bulgarian playwright Yordan Yovkov's most acclaimed works.

There is no real town, nor are there any historical sights, in fact very little to indicate exactly what country you are holidaying in – it is simply an excellent beach resort.

*25km south of Balchik. www.albena.com. Trolleybus transport from hotels to beach. Bus connections with Balchik, Dobrich, Zlatni Pyasutsi, and Varna. Parking charge for vehicles.*

## Ahtopol (Ахторол)

The most southerly point for public transport along the coast, Ahtopol can't be described as a tourist resort (it's too low-key), though it's a good jumping off point for Strandjha Nature Park (*see p141*). The town suffered a devastating fire in 1918, so there are scant historical remains, but Bulgarians enjoy the many holiday homes scattered around the town. Ahtopol has a decent beach but it's a little distance away from the centre of the town.

*80km south of Burgas. Bus connections with Burgas, Kiten and Primorsko.*

## Balchik (Балчик)

Balchik is a town of steep cobbled lanes flanked by quaint whitewashed and

### The Black Sea

The Black Sea borders six countries. Turkey, Ukraine, Russia, Romania and Georgia all share its 4,000km coastline – Bulgaria's portion is a rather meagre 400km.

terracotta-tile-roofed cottages set below white chalk cliffs. An early Roman town closer to the shoreline was wiped out by a tidal wave, probably caused by an earthquake on an Aegean or Turkish fault line, so 'new' Balchik was rebuilt at a higher elevation in the 7th century AD. In 1913 the region around the town was annexed by Romania. It returned to Bulgarian sovereignty in 1940 but this

## The Black Sea Coast

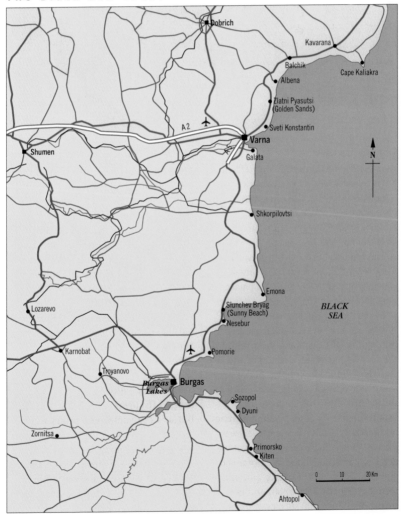

The Italian-style gardens of Queen Marie's Palace, Balchik

short period of Romanian rule left the town the legacy of its greatest attraction – the Summer Palace of Queen Marie (*3km west of town on the E87; tel: (0579) 72 559; open daily 8am–8pm; admission charge*).

The English-born Queen, consort to King Ferdinand of Romania, wanted a retreat from court life and this palace, built in the early 1920s, was perfect. Set in 35 hectares the palace is made up of several separate modest villas set at different height levels and distance from the sea with a stream, a waterfall and a church all linked by cobbled pathways – rather like a small village. One villa was for the use of the royal couple while others offered space for guests, courtiers and servants. An Italianate garden was planted along the seafront with seating areas to enjoy the views. The botanical gardens that grace the palace grounds were developed in the 1950s and now incorporate over 500 species of plant.

The palace and gardens host an annual arts festival in early July.

In the town itself there are a couple of small but interesting museums. The History Museum (*pl. Nezavisimost 1; tel: (0579) 72 177; open Mon–Fri 9am–noon and 1pm–4pm; admission charge*) has some fine ancient Greek and Roman statues, while the Ethnological Museum (*ul. Vitosha 3; tel: (0579) 72 177; open Mon–Fri 8am–noon and 1.30pm–5.30pm; admission charge*) displays local handicrafts and traditional costumes. *49km north of Varna. Bus connections with Varna, Dobrich and Albena.*

## Burgas (Бургас)

Bulgaria's principal port and its fourth biggest city, Burgas (also spelt Bourgas) is a thriving commercial centre. The Thracians and Romans settled here because of the mineral springs, but Burgas really took off in the late 1800s when the railway arrived.

Hemmed in to the coastline by the expansive Burgas Lakes (*see next page*) the suburbs have grown up rather than out, characterised by dour socialist apartment blocks. But the centre of town still has several attractions worth visiting and its tree-lined avenues and several pedestrianised boulevards make it a pleasure to stroll around.

The small Archaeological Museum (*ul. Aleko Bogoridi 21; tel: (056) 843 541; open summer Mon–Fri 8am–noon and 1pm–5pm, winter Tue–Sat 9am–noon and 2pm–5pm; admission charge*) displays finds from throughout the town's history, concentrating on the Roman era but including the only wooden Thracian tomb found along the coast.

Brakalov House is home to Burgas Ethnological Museum (*ul. Slavyanska 69; tel: (056) 842 586; open Mon–Fri 8am–noon and 1pm–5pm; admission*

*charge*). It has displays of costumes, furniture and traditional arts and crafts dating from the late 19th century when the house belonged to Burgas mayor Dimitar Brakalov. The upper floors have some colourful costumes used in traditional Bulgarian folk dances but all information in the museum is in Cyrillic only.

Burgas Art Gallery (*ul. Mitropolit Simeon 24; open Mon–Fri 9am–noon and 2pm–6pm; admission charge*), unusually housed in an early 20th-century former synagogue, has an interesting collection of contemporary art by Bulgarian artists, juxtaposed with a small collection of icons.

Between the town and the sea lies Maritime Park, the place where everyone goes to relax or take an evening stroll. With a mixture of formal and informal spaces dotted with sculptures and

One of the many excursion boats that ply the Black Sea coast

Burgas Lakes, an important wetland reserve

several cafés, it is also the venue for many activities during Burgas' cultural festivals, the principal event being the International Folklore Festival in late August.

*110km south of Varna. Bus connections with Ahtopol, Kiten, Nesebur, Pomorie, Primorsko, Sozopol, Slunchev Bryag, and Varna. Also connections with many towns in central Bulgaria. Tourist office ul. Lyuben Karavelov 12b. Tel: (056) 81 35 95.*

### Burgas Lakes (Бургаски Езера)

Four large shallow lakes on the landward side of Burgas comprise the largest wetland habitat in Bulgaria. Covering almost 10,000 hectares, it is home to over 170 species of birds but not all of it is protected and it sits uncomfortably beside the fast-growing port and industrial area with all its attendant pollution concerns.

You'll find the Poda Conservation Centre (*Tel: (056) 55 07 18; open daily 9am–6pm; admission charge; bus 5, 17 or 18 from Burgas*) at Lake Mandrensko, around 7km south of Burgas town. The centre co-ordinates all park activities, including guided tours and specialised overnight field trips. From the two viewing platforms at the Poda building you can look out across the lake, the heart of the Poda Protected Area, to spot waders such as ibis or spoonbills or divers such as cormorants, which seem to be the most prolific species – hundreds of their nests adorn numerous nearby power pylons. A 2.5km nature walk (*admission charge*) leads deeper into the park, where it's possible to get a little closer to the birds.

Lake Vaya to the north of Mandrensko is a seawater habitat and summer home to a vast population of migratory

pelicans (best seen Apr–Oct). A boat trip is available (*admission charge*) but arrangements need to be made through the Poda Conservation Centre.
*Buses 17 or 18 to Poda Conservation Centre from Burgas.*

## Cape Kaliakra (Нос Калуакра)

Cape Kaliakra is the northern limit of the tourist infrastructure on the Black Sea coast. Beyond this pointed spur projecting southward into the sea you'll find only a string of tiny villages until you reach the Romanian border. Kaliakra Nature Reserve (Национален Резерват Калуакра) (*see p138*), one of the most important protected areas in the country for sea birds and mammals, covers much of the cape.
*70km north of Varna. Bus connections with Balgarevo 8km from the tip.*

## Dobrich (Добрич)

Though 30km or so inland from the Black Sea coast, Dobrich is included here because it's a popular and easy day trip from the resorts. During the communist era, Dobrich was renamed Tolbuhin in honour of a Soviet general. Celebrated throughout Bulgaria for its arts and crafts – at its peak it had over 300 workshops – today it is the Stariyat Dobrich Complex (*ul. Konstantin Stoilov; open daily summer 8am–6pm, winter 8am–5pm; admission free; guided tours in English available for a charge*) that everyone comes to visit. This tiny quarter of the town – a series of cobbled alleyways – has been transformed into an arts and crafts commune with potters, weavers and printers beavering away in their studios and it is one of the best places in Bulgaria to buy genuine

Helpful information at Cape Kaliakra

Dobrich Ethnological Museum

The remains of Roman Nesebur are very much in evidence

artisan-crafted souvenirs. You can ponder which purchases you want to make in one of several cafés amongst the galleries or in the streets off pl. Svoboda. This huge square is typically socialist in its design, surrounded by high apartment blocks and sombre public buildings.

For an insight into the National Revival era visit the pretty Ethnological Museum (*ul. 25 Septemvri; open Mon–Fri 9am–noon and 2pm–5pm*), an 1861 mansion with displays of the 19th-century lifestyles of many regions of Bulgaria.
*55km northwest of Albena. Bus connections with Balchik, Varna and Ruse.*

### Kiten (Китен)
Set amongst beachside forests at the southern end of Primorsko Bay, Kiten

was abandoned after the fall of the Turks. Not so much a resort as a fragmented collection of buildings, it sits on the marshy mouth of the Karaagach River. This section of coast is pretty much out of the mainstream, excellent for those who want a quieter stay and a more 'Bulgarian' feel. The beach (*see p123*) is certainly the highlight of the town.
*55km south of Burgas. Bus connections with Primorsko and Ahtopol.*

### Nesebur (Несебър)
Probably the one place everybody should visit when they come to the Bulgarian Black Sea, Nesebur (also spelled Nesebâr) is a delightful old town clinging limpet-like to the shell of a narrow rocky isthmus protected by the remnants of once-sturdy ancient Greek

and Roman walls. Nesebur is famed for its unique ensemble of Romanesque churches and its fine National Revival mansions, so much so that the town has been designated a World Heritage Site by UNESCO. The downside of it being a must see attraction is that everyone else wants a piece of the action too – the town is full of day-trippers by late morning. To get the best out of Nesebur arrive early, or stay overnight and enjoy the peace and quiet after the tour buses have departed.

Traces of the early Thracian and Greek settlement of Mesembria now lie below sea level but the Romans built on what is now Nesebur isthmus. As part of the Byzantine Empire from the 5th century it prospered as a trading port

and fortress but during the latter years of Byzantine rule became a pawn between Constantinople and the Bulgarian Empire, changing hands several times. Each new ruler felt the need to stamp his mark and it was at this time that most of the over 40

### Ride like the Wind
Just south of Kiten lies Atliman Bay (Bay of the Horse), so named during the Ottoman era. Legend tells us that a young concubine escaped from the well-guarded harem in the Topkapi Palace in Istanbul. She was eventually recaptured, but the Sultan was so impressed by her guile and bravado that he offered her freedom wherever her horse could ride within the day. She rode north of the city then west along the Black Sea coast to reach the Atliman Bay, and liberty.

The harbour at Nesebur

One of Nesebur's Romanesque churches

churches were erected, each trying to outshine the others. During Turkish rule the fortifications were strengthened but the town declined in importance, only to rise phoenix-like during the Bulgarian National Revival period. Today it thrives again, on a lifeblood of tourism.

Just on the right after you enter the old town through the impressive remnants of the ancient city walls, the Archaeological Museum (*ul. Mesembria 2; open May–Sept Mon–Fri 9am–7pm; Sat–Sun 9am–noon and 1pm–7pm, Oct–Apr Mon–Fri 9am–noon and 1pm–5pm; admission charge*) is an excellent place to start your tour. It displays a range of ancient and Byzantine artefacts and a collection of icons salvaged from the town's numerous churches and chapels.

Ul. Mesembria forms the arterial route through the town and one can wander along the narrow alleyways that feed from it. The streets are bedecked with traditional lace; almost every house is a souvenir shop.

Nesebur once boasted over 70 churches. Many are now sadly neglected, but they still form one of the most important collections of Romanesque religious architecture in the world. A selection of icons and murals have been rescued from the ruins, to be displayed in the town Archaeological Museum and the Icon Museum in Sofia (*see pp38–9*). Only one, the Nesebur Orthodox Church (*ul. Slavyanska*), still functions as a place of worship.

The Pantokrator Church (*ul. Mesembria*) is the first church you'll see as you travel up into the town from the museum, and it's perhaps most useful as a guide to the 'Nesebur style', with its red and white striped exterior, domes and columns. The interior has now been converted into a commercial gallery. The imposing remains of the Basilica (also known as the Metropolitan Church) (*ul. Mesembria*) are the largest in the town. Erected in the 9th century on the site of a 6th-century church, it was the seat of the region's bishop, a very rich repository until 1257, when its treasures were looted by the Venetians.

St Stefan's Church (*ul. Ribarska. Open May–Sept daily 9am–1pm and 2pm–6pm, closed Oct–Apr; admission charge*) was completed in the 12th century and took over the bishopric after the Basilica was ransacked. The three-naved interior exhibits some fine 15th- and 16th-century murals typical of the so-called Nesebur School. The exterior is also decorated with an unusual frill of ceramic and enamel tiles, which represent a development in architectural style at the time. The Church of St John the Baptist (*ul. Mitropolitska*), erected in the 10th century, has recently been renovated and also houses a gallery, but should be visited for the well-preserved 14th-century murals that adorn two of the walls. A later artistic style can be seen in the remaining frescoes at St Todor Church (*ul. Neptun*) but, sadly, it's rarely open to the public. Though the Church of St John Aliturgetos now lies in ruins after an earthquake in 1913, it probably has the most romantic setting of any church in the town.

Although the churches are without doubt the archaeological highlight of

Nesebur, later National Revival buildings now shape the town, offering some of the finest vistas of their kind in eastern Bulgaria. The Ethnological Museum (*ul. Mesembria 34; open May–Oct daily 10am–2pm and 3pm–6pm, closed Nov–Apr; admission charge, free on Sat*) is a case in point. Set in a typical National Revival house, it displays a range of national and folk costumes and traditional fabrics.

*35km north of Burgas. Bus connections with Burgas, Varna and Slunchev Bryag (Sunny Beach). Don't park just outside the town walls, or you will be towed away. Park your car in the car park just before the isthmus and walk the 300m into the old town.*

### Pomorie (Поморие)

Destroyed by fire in 1906, Pomorie is a shadow of its former self. The shallow bay to the north of town with its inshore lake and natural sand spit is one of the best locations on the coast for wind and kite surfing. The town beach isn't bad but the tourism infrastructure lags behind other resorts on this part of the coast.

*20km north of Burgas. Bus connections with Burgas, Nesebur, and Slunchev Bryag.*

### Primorsko (Приморско)

Primorsko is a lower key resort than those north of Burgas, seeing more Bulgarian visitors than foreign tourists. The curved sheltered beach is an attraction but there's little else to see here.

*50km south of Burgas. Buses to Burgas and Kiten.*

Ropotamo's sand dunes

### Ropotamo Nature Reserve
### (Национален Резерват Ропотамо)
*See p139.*

### Slunchev Bryag (Сльнчев Бряг)

The largest purpose-built resort on the
Black Sea coast, the site of Sunny Beach,
as it's known in English (also spelt
Slânchev Bryag), was chosen because of
its excellent strand (*see p122*). Over 100
hotels offer just about everything
families need for a perfect package
holiday and many are set in ample
grounds with pools and sports facilities.
Its only role is as a package destination –
so much so that the whole place pretty
much closes down between October and
April. There's little genuine Bulgarian
charm here. Most holidaymakers try to
find that by taking day trips to nearby
Nesebur (it's a pleasant walk from one
to the other along the beach).

*5km north of Nesebur. Bus connections
with Burgas, Nesebur, Pomorie and
Varna.*

### Sozopol (Созорол)

Rivalling Nesebur in its character
(though not in architectural
importance), old Sozopol is a
characterful cluster of National Revival
houses set on narrow cobbled streets. It's
home to a thriving artistic community
and its good town beaches and lively
nightlife make it the best all-round
resort on the Black Sea.

It was first inhabited by the Thracians
from 4000BC and they were joined by
the Greeks in around 600BC; the
combined populations thrived on trade
until the town, then named Apollonia,
was razed by Roman forces in 72BC.
Though it revived later under Roman
occupation it fell into decline following

the fall of the Empire and spent much of the last millennium as a simple fishing village. Sozopol was abandoned following the Russian-Turkish War (1878), when the population feared Turkish reprisals. It was many decades before it was resettled.

There are few specific attractions here. The Archaeological Museum (*ul. Han Krum 2; open summer daily 8am–5pm, winter Mon–Fri 8am–noon and 1pm–5pm; admission charge*) has some finds discovered by marine biologists just offshore, and the Art Gallery (*ul. Kiril & Metodii 70; open Tue–Sat 8am–noon and 2pm–6pm; admission charge*) has a collection of seascapes. However, many of Sozopol's buildings now house bars, cafés and shops and it's the perfect place for a stroll on a warm summer evening.

Sozopol street

Tourism has replaced fishing as Sozopol's main source of income

Just offshore from Sozopol is St John's Island, now an uninhabited nature reserve covering over 650 hectares. You can visit by boat from the Kraybrezhna quayside (*admission charge*) and bird watch or explore the remains of a ruined Byzantine monastery. *30km south of Burgas. Bus connections with Burgas, Ahtopol, Primorski and Kiten.*

### Strandjha Nature Park (Национален Парк Странджа)
*See p141.*

### Sveti Konstantin (Свети Константин)
Founded just after the Second World War on a source of mineral springs, the resort of Sveti Konstantin was originally called Drubzha, meaning Friendship, but today takes its name from the tiny church of Sveti Konstantin and Sveti Elena (Св Константин н Св Елена), built in the 18th century in the centre of town. A number of hotel spa complexes sit amongst pine forests and here you can enjoy massages and other forms of treatment (*see pp164–5*). There's also a reasonable beach.

*10km north of Varna. Bus connections with Varna; also Varna to Zlatni Pyasutsi buses will stop at Sveti Konstantin.*

### Varna (Варна)
Varna, Bulgaria's third largest city, is the major conurbation of the Black Sea coast. Its position on the mouth of the Varnensko estuary, backed by the rolling hills of the Frangensko Plateau, has been coveted as far back as 4000BC, when the Thracians founded the first settlement here. However it was the Romans who really put Varna (then called Odessos) on the map.

In the late 1800s Varna enjoyed another economic rejuvenation when the railway linked it with Ruse on the Danube, completing an important industrial transport conduit. The

### ROMAN BATHS

Bath complexes were an integral part of the social life of the Roman city at a time when citizens (as opposed to slaves) had lots of free time to fill. No expense was spared in the sophistication of the plumbing, the quality of the building or the interior décor. Along with steam and massage rooms, the *thermae* consisted of a series of rooms; the hot water rooms (*caldarium*), tepid water rooms (*tepidarium*) and cold rooms (*frigidarium*). To gain the most benefit one started with a dip in the *frigidarium*, working through the temperature ranges to the *caldarium*.

Pedestrianised boulevard in Varna

nearby mineral spas and beaches also attracted holidaymakers from the earliest era of tourism. Today it's a cultural highlight of the region, with a multitude of summer festivals and galleries galore.

The Varna Archaeological Museum (*ul. Maria Luisa 41; tel: (052) 681 011; open summer Tue–Sun 10am–5pm, winter Tue–Sat 10am–5pm; admission charge*) is the largest museum in Bulgaria, offering the best display of ancient artefacts in the country. It's a mammoth collection that needs some time to take in fully. The collections are set out chronologically and have English captions, which makes everything easy to follow. Make a point of viewing objects discovered at the Varna Thracian Necropolis, as the complex (west of town) is now closed to the public. The finds, dating from 4000BC, include gold jewellery of amazing workmanship. The Roman galleries are also impressive, despite some finds having been spirited away to Sofia.

The town's Ethnological Museum (*ul. Panagyurishte 22; tel: (052) 650 588; open daily 10am–5pm; admission charge*) brings more recent Bulgarian social history to life. Housed in a National Revival Period mansion of c. 1860, it features furniture from the period. There are displays on winemaking, on the once-thriving fishing industry and on recent but now lost agricultural customs.

The first school in Varna is now home to the Museum of National Revival (*ul. 27 Sedmi Juli; tel: (052) 223 585; open summer Tue–Sun 10am–5pm, winter Tue–Sat 10am–5pm; admission charge*),

Varna Archaeological Museum

which concentrates on the Russian-Turkish War period. The old photographs of Varna are particularly interesting and there is a also large collection of icons to enjoy.

However, not all of Varna's archaeological jewels lie hidden in shady rooms. The largest church in the town is the beautiful Cathedral of the Assumption (*pl. Mitropolitska Simeon*). Completed in 1886 in archetypal Orthodox style, it is decorated with 20th-century frescoes. The much fêted 2nd-century AD Roman Spa (*ul. Khan Krum; open summer Tue–Sun 10am–5pm, winter Tue–Sat 10am–5pm; admission charge*) are a little disappointing. Of the third-largest Roman baths complex so far identified in Europe and certainly the most extensive in Bulgaria, only a fraction remains in reasonable condition. Far more impressive is the

Primorski Park

St Anastasios Orthodox Church (*ul. Graf Ignatiev*), built on top of the spa at its eastern corner in 1602, though the interior was totally renovated after the departure of the Ottomans. The interior is a riot of gilt with a fine iconostasis and some worthy modern icons.

Once you've had your fill of cultural delights, do what the locals do and head for Primorski Park. Almost 100 hectares of woods and gardens runs for 7km along the shoreline of the Black Sea, and in summer there's always something happening – concerts, festivals, and street entertainers – plus the draw of the adjacent beach. Primorski has its own collection of attractions: Zoopark (*daily summer 8am–8pm, winter 8am–5pm; admission charge*) for animals, Terrarium Varna (*daily 9am–6pm; admission charge*) for spiders and such, the

Aquarium (*daily 9am–7pm; admission charge*) and Dolphinarium (*shows at 11am, 2pm and 3.30pm Jun–Aug; admission charge*). You'll also find the largest Naval Museum (*summer Mon–Fri 10am–6pm, winter Mon–Fri 8am–5pm; admission charge*) in Bulgaria here, with a motley collection of old and tired vessels.

*110km north of Burgas. Varna Airport is the main point of entry for domestic scheduled and international charter flights. Buses to points across Bulgaria; local connections with Burgas, Dobrich, Nesebur and Slunchev Bryag.*

### Zlatni Pyasutsi (Златни Пясьци)

Called Golden Sands in English, this modern purpose-built resort (also spelt Zlatni Pyasâtsi) is set on one of the best beaches along the coast (*see p122*). One of only a handful of resorts that takes the majority of its holidaymakers from abroad, it has little Bulgarian character but good facilities for a beach-based holiday.

Close to the resort is Aladzha Monastery (Аладжа Манастир) (*open summer Tue–Sun 9am–6pm, winter Tue–Sat 9am–4pm; admission charge*) a complex of caves carved out of the rocky cliffs backing the resort during the early years of Ottoman occupation. The caverns (signposted 'Catacombs') lie up to 40m above ground level and are reached by a series of ladders and stairways; they are decorated with interesting, though faded, murals. The small museum on site explains how the caves were carved. *20km north of Varna. Bus connections with Varna.*

Varna's Cathedral of the Assumption

# Drive: The Southern Black Sea Coast

This drive allows you to break out of the man-made resort of Slunchev Bryag (Sunny Beach) to discover some of the natural and historic sites of the southern coast. It's a full day of activities but you are never far from refreshment to keep your energy levels high, and you can always cool down at one of the many beaches en route if the day gets too hot for sightseeing.

*Distance: 180km; allow 8 hours.*

*Leave the resort on the main E87/A9 road. Just beyond the southernmost hotels of the resort there is a left turn to Nesebur which leads through the modern part of town to the isthmus, where you'll see the old part of town. Park in the large car park on the right just before the causeway that links the isthmus to the mainland.*

## 1 Nesebur (Несебър)

This is one of the cultural highlights of the entire country and a UNESCO World Heritage site. Stroll along the cobbled lanes to enjoy the pretty 19th-century mansions and explore the numerous Romanesque churches. Nesebur is also a great place to buy your holiday souvenirs.

*After Nesebur, head south on the coast road (E87/A9) in the direction of Burgas (Бургас). After 22km it's possible to take a left turn to the resort of Pomorie, with its excellent windsurfing, but this drive takes you on to the more impressive highlights. Continue on the main E87/A9 road.*

## 2 Burgas Lakes

Ten kilometres south of Pomorie you'll pass between the two northerly Burgas Lakes, a rich environment for bird life. Keep a watch out for huge flocks of pelicans, several species of gulls and wading birds such as spoonbills.

*Seventeen kilometres south of Pomorie on the main E87/A9 you'll arrive in the centre of Burgas.*

## 3  Burgas

Burgas is a large town but has some pleasant pedestrianised streets to facilitate exploration. Visit the Archaeological and Ethnological museums before heading to the shade of Maritime Park.

*Pick up the E87/A9 south of the town (signposted Sozopol/Созорол) to continue your journey. Seven kilometres out of town look out for a small building on the left marked PODA.*

## 4  Burgas Lakes Visitor Centre

This is the visitor centre for the Burgas Lakes complex. There's a small display on the bird life you can see on the lakes (not all species inhabit the lakes all year round) but the highlight is the view across the marshes of the southern lakes from its observation platforms. Binoculars are supplied to help you get a bird's-eye view.

*Continue south another 20km to Sozopol (Созорол).*

## 5  Sozopol

Perhaps the most 'rounded' of the Black Sea resorts, Sozopol has a little bit of everything. This is the perfect place to have lunch or a cooling drink surrounded by National Revival architecture in the old town or by the pretty town beach.

*From Sozopol it's only 10km south to the Ropotamo National Park (Национален Резерват Ропотамо).*

## 6  Ropotamo National Park

This park protects vast natural marshes that form an important environment for rare flora and fauna, including desert orchids. The sand dunes here are the most extensive in Bulgaria. Enjoy a boat trip or a walk around the public area of the park and then head just to the north to the tiny resort of Dyuni. You can spend some time on the beach here while you decide whether to extend your journey south to the smaller resorts of Kiten (Китен) and Ahtopol (Ахторол), and finally to the remote Strandjha Nature Park (Национален Парк Странджа) hugging the border with Turkey (an extra 100km return), or head north back to Sunny Beach.

Burgas Lakes Visitor Centre

# Walk: Central Varna

Varna makes the perfect excursion destination: lots to see and pleasant, mostly pedestrian-only, streets to link the various attractions. Primorski Park is a great place to break your trip, especially if you have children, and there are lots of cafés to stop at for an excellent fortifying Bulgarian coffee. *This 4km walk will take about 4 hours (longer if you linger in the park or at the beach).*

## 1 Archaeological Museum

Start at the neo-classical Archaeological Museum, the largest in the country, with a comprehensive range of ancient artefacts. You could easily spend a couple of hours here!
*From the museum walk right along bul. Maria Luisa (вул Мариа Луиса) and after 300m you'll reach pl. Metropolit Simeon (пл Метрополит Симеон).*

## 2 Cathedral of the Assumption

On your right, the domes and arches of the Cathedral of the Assumption come into view. This is arguably Bulgaria's finest 19th-century urban church outside Sofia and is an emblem of the town. Some interesting 20th-century icons grace the interior. The pretty gardens around the church square are one of the best places to buy

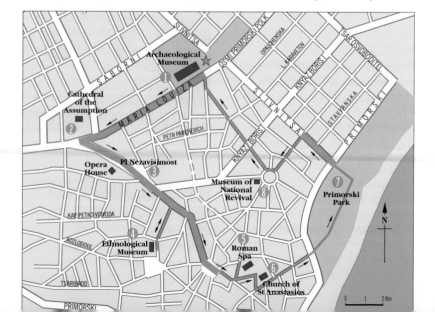

traditional lace souvenirs. The 50 or so lady stallholders sit making new pieces while they display their tablecloths and napkins. You'll also find a small selection of flea-market-style stalls.

*From the cathedral, take the underpass under four-lane bul. Maria Luisa to reach the top of pedestrian street ul. Preslav (ул Презлав). Walk down Preslav for around 50m to pl. Nezavisimost (пл Независимост).*

### 3 Ploshtad Nezavisimost

This pleasant tree-lined square is lined with shady cafés. Look out for the cupola of Varna Opera House on your right as you enter the square.

*Continue down ul. Preslav. Another major pedestrian thoroughfare, bul. Knyaz Boris III (вул Кнйаз Борис III), heads off left (with some good modern shopping opportunities), but carry on until you find ul. Panayurishte (ул Панагюрище) on the right (the first main street after Knyaz Boris III). At the intersection of the next junction you'll find the Ethnological Museum.*

### 4 Ethnological Museum

This National Revival mansion is furnished with period pieces. It presents a perfect opportunity to step back into one of Bulgaria's heydays.

*Retrace your steps back to ul. Preslav and take a right to a small square. Straight across the square is ul. San Stefano (ул ст Стефано). Take this and the first junction left, ul. Khan Krum (ул Хан Крум), to find the entrance to the Roman Spa.*

### 5 Roman Spa

This half-excavated complex gives an impression of just what delights remain under the modern city, but it's not well captioned. The vaulted complex is one of the largest of its kind yet found in Europe.

### 6 St Anastasios Church

Above the baths is the church of St Anastasios (*ul. Graf Ignatiev/*ул Граф Игнатиев), with its ultra-ornate Orthodox interior.

*From the church walk left down ul. Graf Ignatiev, then cross busy ul. Primorski (ул Приморски) to enter Primorski Park.*

### 7 Primorski Park

*Once you've explored the park or spent some time on Varna's adjacent town beach, take the main park entrance out back into the town. This pedestrianised area, forming a bridge over ul. Primorski, leads into an open square with the modern Festival Hall on your left and bul. Slivnitsa (вул Слвница) straight ahead. Walk up Slivnitsa, then turn left at ul. Stefan Karadzha (ул Стефан Караджа) to reach pl. Ekzarh Josif (пл Екзах Йусиф), where you'll find the Museum of National Revival.*

### 8 Museum of National Revival

The many aspects of Bulgarian Nationalism are explored here, including local involvement in the Russian-Turkish War, but the icons are probably the most interesting attraction to non-Bulgarian visitors.

*From the museum take a left up ul. 25 Juli (ул 25 Юли) and cross bul. Maria Luisa to find yourself back at the Archaeological Museum.*

# Black Sea Beaches

The Black Sea is famed for its beaches. But it isn't one long stretch of sand from north to south. Here's some information to help you make your choice.

## Major Resorts

The 'big three' resorts anchor tourism on the Black Sea. This is where the major action is if you want plenty of bars and restaurants. You'll also have lots of company, especially in July and August.

**Albena** is the most up-market resort. Purpose built on four kilometres of fine golden sand, the beach is exceptionally good for children because it has a wide stretch of coastal shallows so they can paddle and swim in relative safety. There are also plenty of watersports. There are around 50 hotels within the complex. Much of the resort is traffic free and there's a long seafront promenade lined with restaurants, bars and cafés.

**Slunchev Bryag** (Sunny Beach) has probably the longest beach along the coast, a magnificent 8km of sand over 100m wide: the perfect location for a holiday resort. There are excellent facilities for families and young children. Most of the 100 or so hotels crowd the southern half of the beach and walking a couple of kilometres north gives you more space.

**Zlatni Pyasutsi** (Golden Sands) is now the largest resort along the coast and its beach is beautiful, though at 3.7km long it's only half the length of Sunny Beach and caters to about the same number of hotels.

## Smaller Resorts

The travel brochures also feature several other less manufactured resorts.

**Sozopol** has a good sand beach in the town but it's rather small, so you'll need to arrive early to get a decent sun-bed.

**Sveti Konstantin**'s beach is not one long continuous stretch of sand but rather smaller coves broken by rocky outcrops.

**Pomorie**'s town beach is broken by a series of groynes (wooden barriers) designed to stop the sand from being eroded by the sea. It is sandy but narrow and it does get very busy.

## Quieter Resorts

Those who want less crowded beaches and perhaps a more genuinely Bulgarian atmosphere have several options.

**Ahtopol** is a relaxed resort in the south set on a cape flanked by two long sandy beaches. The northern one is renowned throughout Eastern Europe as a nudist beach. About 5km south of the town is the outlet of the Veleka River, barred by a sandy spit offering seawater swimming to the east and cooler freshwater swimming in the river to the west.

**Kiten,** also in the south, sits close to the beautiful horseshoe-shaped Atliman Beach, with its exceptional azure blue shallows.

Two smaller resorts between Varna and Burgas are **Byala** and **Obzor**. If you want a low-key cosy resort with a few eateries combined with a good beach then these are ideal.

For the ultimate in 'get away from it all' Black Sea coast beaches, you'll need to head south into Strandjha Nature Park. This protected corner of Bulgaria hugs the Turkish border. There is little in the way of tourist infrastructure there but you'll definitely be rewarded by totally unspoilt strands. Silistar Beach is the best. Blessed with golden sand and shallow azure waters, it's still relatively unknown – you'll just have to hurry before the secret gets out!

Facing page: Albena resort
This page: Sunny Beach view

# Northern Bulgaria

Visitors tend to forsake the north for the more obvious delights south and east of Sofia, leaving much of the area north of the Stara Planina Mountains remarkably free of foreign tourists. But Bulgaria's least visited region has several worthy attractions, including exceptional fortifications, important and unspoiled natural landscapes, and the most renowned rock tomb in the country.

Cherepish Monastery

### Belogradchik (Белоградчик)

Set dramatically amongst immense red rock formations the name of Belogradchik is derived from the Bulgarian *beliya gradezh*, the white building, after the strong granite fortress that dominates the modern town.

Founded by the Romans and expanded by the Byzantines, the citadel (*open daily 8am–5pm; admission charge*) was occupied throughout Bulgaria's history until the 18th century because it protected the northern route towards what is now Romania. In 1850 a localised peasant uprising was brutally put down by the Ottomans. The last few rebels were slaughtered in the citadel. Much of what you see today is 17th-century Ottoman. Magnificent buttress walls and fine tower entrance portals – this is how a castle should look.

The old quarter of the town below is gradually being renovated under the Beautiful Bulgaria Project (*see p55*) but it is still work in progress. Head to the History Museum (*pl. 1850 Leto; open 8am–noon and 1.30pm–5.30pm; admission charge*) for assorted artefacts found at the fortress and geological information about the Belogradchik rocks.

*52km south of Vidin. Bus connections with Vidin and Montana.*

### Cherepish Monastery (Черепишски Манастир)

Nestling on the banks of the Iskur River at the foot of the high curtain walls of the river valley, Cherepish is one of the smallest and most peaceful monasteries in Bulgaria. The retreat has gruesome antecedents, founded after a bloody 14th-century battle won by Tsar Ivan Shishman. It is said that he ordered the skulls of the dead to be piled high and ordained that a monastery should be founded on that very spot. Cherepish is derived from *cherep*, the Bulgarian word for skull. The monastery was the subject of a number of raids by Ottoman forces and was the leading Haidouk refuge (*see pp78–9*) in the northwest.

The monastery has few important religious relics, though the church has a set of three works by Patriarch Evtimii and written documents dating from the

15th century. It is much more the atmosphere and setting here that is the attraction. Just outside the walls the monastery has built three blocks of simple rooms and this is one of the best places in Bulgaria to enjoy a few days of peace and contemplation.

*70km north of Sofia. Open daily 8am–8pm. Admission free. Buses from Sofia to Vratsa will stop on the main road 1km from the monastery entrance.*

### Cherven (Червен)

Set on the very southern tip of one of the spurs of the Rusenski Lom National Park, Cherven is a tiny settlement now opening up to tourism because of the medieval citadel overlooking the valley. One of the best preserved of its type in the Balkans and used as a template for restorations taking place at Tsarevets Fortress in Veliko Turnovo (*see p70*), the citadel – an important trading and defensive town during the 13th and 14th centuries – has the remains of the city walls, streets, churches and the inner fortifications.

Cherven's medieval citadel

*40km south of Ruse. Open daily 9am–noon and 2pm–5pm. Bus connections with Ruse.*

### Northern Bulgaria

## Ivanovo Rock Monastery
## (Скален Манастир Иваново)

Bulgaria's most famous cave monastery, Ivanovo (officially the St Archangel Michael Monastery) was hewn out of the cliffs above the Rusenski River during the 1400s with funds supplied directly from the Bulgarian royal family. This royal patronage allowed the best artisans to be employed in the decoration of the interior and on the murals by the Turnovo School in the church of St Bogoroditsa (the Holy Virgin), which constitute the major visitor attraction and are considered the best in the Balkans, particularly the evocative *Last Supper*. The church is on the UNESCO World Heritage Site list but is in a poor state of repair, with several sections of the roof looking rather fragile.

*20km south of Ruse. Open Wed–Sun 9am–noon and 1pm–6pm. Admission charge. Bus connections from Ivanovo village, 4km from the site, to Ruse.*

## Ruse (Русе)

Set on Bulgaria's northeastern border on the banks of the Danube, Ruse was first settled by the Romans but it wasn't important again to Bulgarians until the railway arrived. When the Ruse to Varna line opened in 1866, completing the Black Sea–Danube conduit, it vastly increasing trade and boosted the economy of the whole country, but the money and commerce were concentrated here.

When the Ottomans left Bulgaria, Ruse was the country's most prosperous city and its architecture is influenced by the styles fashionable in the Austro-

Ivanovo Rock Monastery

Hungarian Empire to the north, with which it mainly traded. Ploshtad Svoboda at the heart of the town demonstrates this well and is perhaps the finest square in Bulgaria, flanked by neo-Classical facades – look particularly for Dohodnoto Zdanie (the Profitable Building) erected in 1902. The Monument to Freedom erected in 1908 sits at its heart, surrounded by a small park where locals spend their lunchtimes and while away the warm summer evenings.

The Museum of Urban Life (*ul. Tsar Ferdinand 36. Tel: (082) 09 97; open Mon–Fri 9am–noon and 2pm–5pm; admission charge; guided tour in English, separate charge*) is a late 19th-century house fully furnished in a style typical of the time with a good collection of contemporary porcelain and glass.

Of course Ruse had its own 19th-century freedom fighters. The family home of Zahari Stoyanov how houses a museum (*bul. Pridunavski 14. Tel: (082) 09 96; open Mon–Fri 9am–noon and 2pm–5pm; admission charge*) paying homage to the man, who was also a politician and writer. It adds some further background to the history of the liberation movement. In the east of the city, the gardens of Revivalists' Park surround the Pantheon of the National Revival, which commemorates the revolutionary leaders and local people who lost their lives during the Bulgarian liberation.

The oldest church in the city is the Sveta Troitsa (*pl. Sveta Troitsa*). Designed in Russian style, it has some fine 16th-century murals. The (Catholic) Church of St Paul the Crucified (1890) has the country's earliest organ, installed in 1907.

Though the Danube is a mighty river it plays little part in the daily lives of the people. A badly tended waterfront park is spoilt by the proximity of the railway line. There's only one small boat offering river cruises and the busy waterway is crowded with ugly, rusting industrial barges. However, the oldest railway station in Bulgaria, the original Ruse

station, has now been transformed into a small museum (*ul. Bratya-Obretenov; open daily 10am–noon and 2pm–5.30pm*) relating to rail transport and river transport on the Danube. You can also find remnants of the original 1st-century AD Roman fortress Saxaginta Prista by the waterside (*ul. Tsar Kaloyan 2. Tel: (082) 50 04; open Mon–Fri 9am–noon and 2pm–5pm; admission charge*), including the river docks, towers and sleeping quarters of the legionaries.

### The Friendship Bridge

Despite Bulgaria's long northern river border, Ruse is the only town to have a fixed link with Romania; the rest have ferry connections. The Friendship Bridge was begun in 1949 and opened in 1954. A monumental engineering project, it is 3km long and stands 30m above the river. The bridge was not designed to take pedestrian traffic, so you'll need to ride in a vehicle to travel across it.

Ploshtad Svobada, Ruse

## Rusenski Lom National Park
## (Национален Парк Русенски Лом)
*See p140.*

## Silistra (Силистра)
Silistra sits at the point on the Danube where the river leaves Bulgarian soil, cutting north into Romania. It's been settled since Roman times, when it was given the name Durostorum. The town adopted Christianity early and became an important episcopal centre during the first millennium, but the fortresses in the hills above also bear witness to its role as a guardian of borders throughout the last 1800 years. Silistra was the focal point of many minor military actions between Russian and Turks during the 19th century – the author Tolstoy took part in a siege of the town in 1854. From 1913 until 1940 this part of the country was appropriated by Romania. The town is famed for its apricot brandy, and apricot orchards blanket the surrounding valleys.

The large 19th-century Medzhitabiya Turkish fortress is the most formidable building in town but it's not possible to tour the interior. Much smaller, but equally impressive, is the 4th-century AD Roman tomb discovered in 1942, which is decorated with colourful murals. Other elements of the Roman settlement dot the town. The Archaeological Museum (*bul. Simeon Veliki. Tel: (086) 27 040; open Mon–Fri 8am–noon and 2pm–6pm; admission charge*) displays finds from both locations, together with a rare Thracian chariot.
(*120km east of Ruse. Bus connections with Dobrich, Ruse, Shumen and Varna*).

## Lake Sreburna (Езеро Сребърна)
*See p140.*

## Vidin (Видин)
Set in the northernmost corner of Bulgaria on the banks of the Danube looking across into Romania, Vidin is in the process of being gentrified under the Beautiful Bulgaria Project (*see p55*); its once-fine houses are being brought back to life after decades of neglect. In the 14th century the city and its surrounding environs declared independence from the Second Empire. It fell into Ottoman hands but a local tribal lord rebelled in the early 19th century, seeking assistance from Napoleon. Even today its people are considered a little aloof from the rest of the Bulgarian population.

Set on one of the Danube's easier crossing sites it was settled by the Romans, who built a fort to protect the northern border. During the Second Bulgarian Empire it resumed this role and Baba Vida Fortress (*ul. Baba Vida; open daily 8.30am–5pm; admission charge*), now dominating the town, was built. One of the most splendid and complete in the Balkans, the fortress was built at various stages from the 10th to the 14th century, though the Turks consolidated the walls in the 17th century. Because of its rebellion and

### Locked Out
Two Russian generals stole the key to the fortress at Silistra in 1810 during one of the Russian army's regular skirmishes with the Turks. It was taken to St Petersburg, where it remained until 1958 before being ceremonially handed back into the safe hands of Silistra town officials.

semi-independence Vidin was spared the fighting during the Russian-Turkish War and the fort was undamaged. The Austro-Hungarian Habsburgs usurped it for a short period in the 19th century.

Back in town, the Archaeological Museum (*ul. Targovska; open Tue–Sat 9am–noon and 2pm–5.30pm; admission charge*) has a comprehensive collection of Neolithic finds from the local region and Roman artefacts from Vidin itself and from the site of Ratiaria 25km to the south.

*100km north of Montana. Bus connections with Belogradchik, Montana, and Pleven.*

## Vratsa (Враца)

Ignore the grey industrial suburbs that surround the centre of Vratsa. When you get to the heart of the town you'll find tree-lined boulevards, pedestrianised streets with shops and cafés and a large central square, perfect for an afternoon or evening stroll.

The town is often used as a base for hiking and climbing in the Vrachanska Balkan National Park just to the west of town and there are several monasteries in close proximity.

Revered Bulgarian freedom fighter Hristo Botev (*see p79*) was killed close by during the uprising, and the town makes the most of the connection. The main square is named after him and sports a monument to him; confusingly for strangers to the town there's a bul. (boulevard), an ul. (street) and also a pl. (square) Hristo Botev. The Historical Museum (*pl. Hristo Botev. Tel: (092) 20 373; open summer Tue–Sun 9am–1pm and 3pm–6pm, winter Tue–Fri*

One of Vratsa's graceful boulevards

*9am–noon and 2pm–6pm; admission charge*) has a section concerning Botev but is more worthy for its range of displays that include some good Thracian artefacts and items produced by Vratsa goldsmiths, an important industry during the 19th century.

Vratsa's Ethnological Museum Complex (*ul. General Leonov. Tel: (092) 20 209; open Tue–Sun 9am–noon and 3pm–7pm; admission charge*) comprises several National Revival buildings whose highlights include a good collection of national costumes. Kemara, the old craftsman's quarter in the south of the town, is currently being renovated and will house modern artisans once completed.

*116km north of Sofia. Train and bus connections with Sofia and Vidin.*

# Walk: Downtown Ruse

The centre of Ruse reveals grand neoclassical architecture of a kind not usually found in Bulgaria outside the capital. This 3km walk, taking about 3 hours, starts at and is centred on the main square in the town, pl. Svoboda (пл Свобода) or Freedom Square.

### 1 Ploshtad Svoboda

Arguably the finest plaza in Bulgaria, this is the hub of the city and we'll keep returning to it throughout our walk. You'll find several cafés here if you want to take a break along the way. The formal gardens at its centre provide a welcome place for young and old to meet, under the shadow of the Monument to Freedom, erected in 1908 to commemorate the founding of the Bulgarian state. The most splendid building on the square is the Dohodnoto Zdanie (the Profitable Building) erected in 1902. Unfortunately most of it lies empty at the moment; the only section that is occupied belongs to a fast food restaurant. Other fine examples of architecture include the

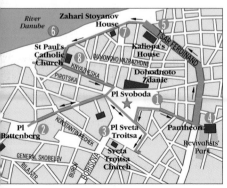

Girdap building, once headquarters of Bulgaria's first private bank, founded in 1881.

*Leave pl. Svoboda by bul. Aleksandrovska (бул Александер) (as this street cuts right across the square, to make sure you are heading in the right direction keep the Law Courts building to your right) and follow the street until you reach pl. Battenberg (пл Баттенберг).*

### 2 Ploshtad Battenberg

Once the main square of the city, Battenberg also displays some fine late 19th- and early 20th-century facades, though it isn't as well kept as pl. Svoboda. Look particularly for the Town Museum, the boys' high school and the Lyuben Karavelov Library, once the city Chamber of Commerce.

*Return to pl. Svoboda and leave it by pl. Sveta Troitsa (пл Света Троица) (keep the municipal building to your right).*

### 3 Ploshtad Sveta Troitsa

Pl. Sveta Troitsa has two important buildings. The Sveta Troitsa Church is the oldest in Ruse, completed in 1632, and the Ruse Opera House, which opened in 1890, still hosts regular performances.

*Return to pl. Svoboda and leave by ul. Petko Petkov (ул Петко Петков) (to the left of the Danube Plaza Hotel. Cross busy bul. Tsar Osvoboditel (вул Освободител) to reach Revivalists' Park.*

## 4 Revivalists' Park

This was once the city cemetery, where many heroes of the struggle for freedom were buried. In 1978 a small pantheon was built here and the bones of many of the dead re-interred in the building. An eternal flame burns within to remember the dead but the graffiti on the back façade indicates that some young Bulgarians have little respect for the past.

*Return to bul. Tsar Osvoboditel and turn right. Follow the four-lane highway as it becomes bul. Tsar Ferdinand (бул Цар Фердинаид). You'll pass the monument to Stefan Karadzha on the right, erected on the spot where he was hanged by the Turks.*

## 5 Kaliopa's House

Further down on the left just before the road meets the river is Kaliopa's House, home to the Museum of Urban Life.

*Turn left where bul. Tsar Ferdinand meets bul. Pridunavski (вул Придунавски).*

## 6 The Danube

The famous river wends its way eastward just across the railway line. A rather neglected park allows access to the riverbank to watch the industrial barges chugging by.

## 7 House of Zahari Stoyanov

On the landward side of bul. Pridunavski you'll find the House-Museum of Zahari Stoyanov, a prominent revolutionary and politician. *Continue along bul. Pridunavski.*

## 8 St Paul's Church

Further along this boulevard, this Catholic church is the repository of Bulgaria's first church organ.

*Walk a little further along bul. Pridunavski until you reach ul. Knyazheska (ул Кнйажеска). Turn left here and it will lead back to pl. Svoboda, your starting point.*

Architecture in the Austro-Hungarian style dating from Ruse's heyday

# The Danube

The River Danube is one of Europe's great waterways. The very mention of its name conjures up images of genteel cruises past vine-draped sun-drenched hills and the occasional schloss or two accompanied by the dulcet tones of Johann Strauss's stirring waltz. Unfortunately, by the time the river gets to Bulgaria, it's a slightly different story. If the water was ever blue, it certainly isn't today! The detritus of five countries floats past here every day.

Throughout the communist era, the river was viewed principally as a transport route and urban river banks were given over to docks and industrial plant to facilitate deliveries to and from Russia's vast Black Sea Coast, from where cargoes would be transported into the heart of the USSR. The idea that the Danube could be used for pleasure or leisure was anathema to the socialist authorities and they remained staunchly indifferent to its important role as a provider of natural habitat.

Some progress was made in 1983 with the creation of the Sreburna Nature Reserve, protecting the 8,000 hectares of shallow lake with an outlet into the Danube, which is recognised by UNESCO as a World Heritage Site for its wildlife, including millions of migratory birds.

Unfortunately Bulgaria couldn't isolate its section of the Danube from the dangers that other countries posed, and in March 1988 a chemical spillage at Giurgiu in Romania caused an environmental disaster for the lower Danube that the scientists estimated would take 20 years to neutralise. Outraged Bulgarians formed an 'eco-glasnost' pressure group – too late to affect the quality of Danube water – but this group was part of the developing opposition movement that brought the end of communism in Bulgaria a year later.

Today, Bulgaria still doesn't sell its stretch of the Danube well. There are few places to actually enjoy the sort of vista that one might experience on the Seine in Paris, for example. There are

few riverside parks and cafés. Lovers of industrial heritage will enjoy the toing and froing of the huge rusting hulks that carry coal and other raw materials along the river, but for most others there is little allure.

Surprisingly, the beacon of economic hope that membership of the European Union brings has also raised a conundrum for the Danube and a catch-22 for the EU's own reputation as friend to the environment. It is one of the EU's core policies to facilitate and promote the use of environmentally friendly forms of transport. Part of this is to get cargoes onto the water if at all possible and the Danube is seen as fundamental to this aim, as it connects the newly independent countries of the ex-Soviet bloc and Turkey (all possible future EU members) with the heart of Europe.

However, in a river plan announced in 2004 it was clear that the dredging and damming necessary to create the minimum draught needed for modern barges will cause irreparable damage to the remaining marshlands along the river's path, and perhaps the loss of the Sreburna Nature Reserve. Environmentalists are even now preparing for the 'mother of all battles'.

The Danube at Ruse provides more eyesores than vistas, though it is vital to wildlife

# Getting Away From It All

Bulgaria presents many and varied ways to get off the beaten track. Much of the country is unknown to mass tourism and it's easy to slip away from the mainstream, even in large towns. However, it is the country's unspoilt hinterland that is the real treasure. Opportunities for eco-tourism are excellent here and the industry is in its infancy as Bulgaria concentrates on the economic recovery from the fall of communism and the adoption of a market economy.

Hiking trail sign

## BULGARIA'S MOUNTAINS
### Pirin Mountains (Пирин Планина)

Nestling in the very southwestern corner of the country, the Pirin Mountains are famed throughout Bulgaria for their lakes and mineral springs, set amongst dramatic alpine cirques and surrounded by more than mountain peaks. The Pirin National Park (Национален Парк Пирин) at 40,000 hectares is the largest in Bulgaria and is listed by UNESCO because of rare natural features such as tufa towers, the diversity of flora and fauna and the number of rare species, including wild bears.

Though less well known to outsiders for its skiing (*see pp100–101*), Pirin is internationally regarded for its excellent walking trails centred on its main resort Bansko, but also from Popina Luka north of Sandanski in the heart of the range. A cross-range trip can take up to 10 days but shorter routes are also marked.

*Pirin National Headquarters, ul. Bulgaria 4, Bansko. Tel: (07443) 82 04, website www.bg–parks.net.*

*Pirin Tourist Forum. ul. Komitrov 8. Tel: (073) 36795; fax: (073) 35458, website www.pirin–tourism.bg Open Mon–Fri 8.30am–6.30pm, Sat summer only 10am–4pm.*

### Rila Mountains (Рила Планина)

The Rila Mountains, south of Sofia, are the Bulgarians' main playground, with excellent hiking in summer and the best-known resorts for winter sports. Almost every activity mentioned in the Sport and Leisure section (*see pp158–63*) is available here, but there's still enough space to find some peace and quiet.

Rila is a landscape shaped by glacial erosion. Crowned by Mount Musala, the highest peak in the Balkans and the 6th highest in Europe, the region offers landscapes from evergreen forests to alpine pastures and lakes; the upper elevations offer archetypal mountainscapes, many of which are protected by the 27,000-hectare Rila National Park (Национален Парк Рила).

getting away

The summer hiking trails are well marked but some of them are taxing for beginners because of their steep inclines. For good short trails – easy routes not too far from sources of refreshment – try Borovets (using the winter ski slopes routes) or the smaller resort of Maliovitsa ( Мальовица). A network of routes can also be found around the famed Rila Monastery (*see pp90–92*).

*Rila National Park Headquarters, ul. Bistritsa 12b, Blagoevgrad. Tel: (073) 880 537, fax: (073) 81023, website www.rilanationalpark.org.*

**Rodopi Mountains
(Родопи Планина)**
Forming Bulgaria's natural boundary with Greece to the south, the Rodopi Mountains lie in the heartland of the region known in antiquity as Thrace. The name is said by some to come from the pagan goddess Rhodope, though others say the range may be named from the Slavic words *ruda* and *ropa* meaning ore and pit, because mining has been an industry here since the Iron Age.

The range is generally lower in altitude than the Pirin or Rila ranges but is blanketed with expansive virgin pine forests in the north and the karst and granite rocks have led to the formation of vast cave complexes and gorges.

The Rodopi see mild but snowy winters and warm but not hot summers, a climate that combines with the terrain to offer superb hiking and skiing, anchored by the internationally known resort of Pamporovo. It's also the area to

A typical view in the Pirin range

The Rodopi Mountains have dramatic rock formations

go caving, spelunking or potholing, and with rock formations such as Choudnite Mostove (Wonderful Bridges) it's good for climbing, too.

## Stara Planina Mountains (Стара Планина)

The Stara Planina range (also known as the Balkan Mountain range) divides Bulgaria, running east–west through the middle of the country from the Serbian border to the Black Sea. The range is the most ancient in the country: in fact its name is derived from a phrase meaning old mountain. The range has been worn to little more than hills by millennia of erosion, but its highest peak, Mount Botev, rises to 2,376m and it has several peaks over 2,000m lying mostly in the western section.

The Stara Planina are the windiest mountains in Bulgaria, often forming the dividing line between two weather systems; this causes dangerous rushes of air through the mountain passes. Unusually, rainfall is at its highest in June, with least rain falling in February.

It's less easy to get away from it all here, especially in the central section. The attraction is more in the hidden monasteries, traditional lifestyles and the generally more gentle gradients. However, there are two centres of excellence. The dramatic Vratsa and Iskur gorges (*see pp52–3*) in the far west of the range (north of Sofia) are much loved by mountain and free climbers and there are some great hiking trails cutting through the peaks. Vrachanski Balkan National Park (Национален Парк Врачански Балкан) was created in this same region (west of Vratsa) in the late 1980s to protect the karst landscape and 28,000 hectares of forested mountainscape, boasting over 700 species of flora and numerous natural caves.

Hiking possibilities are most comprehensive from the west, though there is a 650km marked route (the longest single route in Bulgaria) along the whole of the Stara Planina ridge (from Mount Kom to Cap Emine on the Black Sea), with regularly sited chalets.

This can take over 4 weeks to complete. *Vrachanski Balkan National Park Information Centre. ul. Ivanka Boteva 1, Vratsa. Tel: (092) 654 73. Open Mon–Fri 9am–noon and 2pm–6.30pm.*

### Bear Sanctuary

There's been a tradition of dancing bears in the Balkans since the Middle Ages but sensibilities about performing animals have changed even here, and in 2002 the government made it illegal to 'exhibit' a bear.

Several owners came forward to hand in animals which were of no economic use and with the help of the Brigitte Bardot Foundation, a 12-hectare sanctuary has been set up close to Belitsa in the Rila Mountains to rehabilitate and protect these unfortunate animals.

Ancient hills of the Stara Planina

## OTHER NATIONAL PARKS
### Blue Rocks National Park (Sinite Kamani/Сините Скали)

The heart of rebel country during Bulgaria's fight for independence from the Turks, Blue Rocks protects a small, once impenetrable corner of the country. Today it's a 90-minute walk to the highest peak but there's also a chair lift for those who can't face the hike, and you can explore the caves that the revolutionary guerrillas used for almost two centuries.

*Chairlift operates summer 7.30am–5.30pm, winter 8am–4pm. Admission charge.*

### Golden Sands National Park (Национален Парк Златни Пясъци)

Fragrant pine forest extending over 1,300 hectares blankets the hillsides of the northern Black Sea coast. This national park is the perfect antidote to the bustle of the coastal resorts. An hour's walk through the heady aroma of pine is Aladzha Monastery (*see p116*), carved out of the rocks in the 12th century but long abandoned.

### Kaliakra Nature Reserve (Национален Резерват Калуакра)

Protecting vast expanses of the coastline, the boundaries of 650-hectare Kaliakra Park extend out into the shallows of the Black Sea to a distance of 500m. The area has become known as the Bay of Birds for its almost 300 native and migratory species, though it is also home to a small number of dolphins and seals – the populations are now thought to be in single figures, so you are unlikely to catch a glimpse of either. The cape consists of high sheer cliffs with spectacular long-range views but

Cape Kaliakra's rocky shore

The shoreline of Kaliakra is beautiful, but access is difficult

there is no safe access to the shoreline. Bring binoculars and you can enjoy hours of bird watching, including breeding colonies clinging to the sheer rock face.

Those less enamoured with ornithology can explore the remains of the Kaliakra citadel, in use from the 4th century BC until the 17th century AD. Much of what still remains is Byzantine. *Kaliakra Information Centre on the main street in Bulgarevo (also spelt Bâlgarevo) village on the approach to the cape. Tel: (0574) 44 24. Open daily 9am–6pm.*

## Ropotamo Nature Reserve
### (Национален Резерват Ропотамо)
One of Eastern Europe's most important marshland wildernesses, the Ropotamo protects 20km of river mouth attracting over 200 species of birds. The sand dunes that separate the marshes from the open ocean are the most extensive in Bulgaria and they are also part of the reserve, forming an important habitat for flora that includes rare sand lilies.

A section of the Ropotamo is designated as parkland, offering short hiking trails and a boat trip along the river to catch a glimpse of the less shy wild creatures, including breeding colonies of egrets and herons, turtles and huge carp.
*The Bulgarian–Swiss Biodiversity Conservation Programme (BSBCP) runs the reserve. Project Ropotamo office, Komplex Meden Rudnik 444, Burgas. Tel: (056) 55 97 97. Website www.bsbcp.org.*

Karst landscape in Rusenski Lom

## Rusenski Lom National Park
### (Национален Парк Русенски Лом)

The three-pronged river valleys of the Rusenski Lom, Beli Lom and Malki Lom rivers form the Rusenski Lom National Park, one of Bulgaria's largest protected wildernesses. The sinuous park covers forested mountains, low rising hills and exceptional karst landscape. This range of natural environments has created a wide variety of habitats for over 170 species of native bird, including great eagle owls, 20 species of bat and over 60 species of mammal, of which 10 species are endangered. It also encompasses over 30 incredible rock-cut churches, of which Ivanovo Monastery (*see p126*) is the highlight, and the second largest cave in Bulgaria, the Orlova Chuka Peshtera (Eagle Peak Cave), just south of the village of Tabachka. The region offers hiking on less well-established routes than the mountain parks and a less formalised tourist infrastructure. *Information centres at the town hall in Ivanovo and at the National Park Office, ul. General Skobelev 7, Ruse. Tel: (082) 228 227.*

## Sreburna Nature Reserve
### (Национален Парк Сребърна)

Listed as a World Heritage Site by UNESCO, Lake Sreburna (also spelled Srebârna) is a slow-flowing freshwater marsh, only 5m deep at its maximum, that drains into the Danube. This shallow depth is the perfect environment for reeds and other water-loving plants, which in turn act as a magnet for water birds. Over 160 species inhabit the reserve, from ducks to cormorants, herons to pelicans. Several are on the endangered list. Many nest on remote reed 'islands' that grow throughout the reserve away from the interference of man.

### Strandjha Nature Park
### (Национален Парк Странджа)
Established as recently as 1995, Strandjha sits on the very southern tip of the Black Sea Coast, stretching to the Turkish border. Little visited because of its remote location, it offers a real chance to experience unspoilt and exceptionally varied landscapes from deciduous forest to excellent beaches and marshy shallows. This range of habitat is home to over 150 species of bird and over 50 species of mammals, the largest and most varied flora and fauna of any park in Bulgaria. The hiking here is easy because the terrain is flat and there are numerous trails ranging from 3km to over 20km.

For those more interested in history than in wildlife there are several ruined Byzantine citadels to explore, now languishing in the foliage. These once formed part of a formidable defensive boundary.

There is little mainstream tourist infrastructure but camping is permitted within its boundaries (but with no facilities); this may be the way to see the park at its best. The village of Bulgari in the north of the park hosts a unique fire-walking festival in early June. Otherwise you'll have much of the Strandjha to yourselves.

### Vitosha National Park
### (Национален Парк Витоша)
*See p46.*

Rusenski Lom is excellent hiking country

# Bird Watching

With its exceptionally varied natural landscape and numerous protected regions, Bulgaria is Europe's richest country in bird life. In addition to its many native birds, the country lies on the direct route for many migratory species that make a pit stop here between their seasonal African and European homes. A total of 397 species have been documented, but spring is the best time to visit for sheer variety, with an average of 220 species on Bulgarian soil.

## Plentiful Species

This is the best place in the world to see wallcreepers (*Tichodroma muraria*), the biggest European populations of masked and lesser grey shrike (*Lanuis nubicus* and *Lanuis minor*), short-toed treecreeper (*Carthia brachydactyla*), Spanish sparrow (*Passer hispaniolensis*), collared flycatcher (*Ficedula parva*), black-headed and rock bunting (*Emberiza melanocephala* and *Emberiza* cia), black-headed wagtail (*Motacilla flava feldegg*), golden oriole (*Oriolus oriolus*), bee-eater (*Merops apiaster*), hoopoe (*Upupa epops*), rose-coloured starling (*Sturnus roseus*), corncrake (*Crex crex*), Syrian woodpecker (*Dendrocopos syriacus*), calandra and short-toed larks (*Melanocorypha calandra* and *Calandrella brachydactyla*) and rock nuthatch (*Sitta neumayer*).

## Rare Species

Species that are rare in the rest of Europe but more numerous here include the pallid swift (*Apus pallidus*), little and spotted crake (*Porzana parva* and *Porzana porzana*), stone curlew (*Burhinus oedicnemus*), collared pratincole (*Glareola pratincola*), gull-billed and Caspian tern (*Gelochelidon nilotica* and *Sterna caspia*), eagle owl (*Bubo bubo*), Scops owl (*Otus scops*) and Tegmalms owl (*Aegolius funereus*), shore lark (*Eremophila alpestris*), rock and blue-rock thrush (*Monticola saxatilis* and *Monticola solitarius*), barred, Sardinian and Orphean warbler (*Sylvia nisoria, Sylvia melanocephala* and *Sylvia hortensis*), nutcracker (*Nucifraga caryocatactes*), rock sparrow (*Petronia petronia*) and dotterel (*Charandrius morinellus*).

## When and Where to Set up your Hide

The Rodopi Mountains are Europe's richest environment for raptor species, autumn being the best time to see them. There are said to be 20,000 common buzzards (*Buteo buteo*), 6,000 honey buzzards (*Pernis apivorus*), 10,000 lesser spotted eagles (*Aquila pomarina*) and a handful of rare Lammergeyer (*Gypaetus barbatus*) scanning the countryside for a tasty mouse or vole.

From August to October you'll be witness to a magnificent show of bird migration around the Burgas Lakes – white and black stork (*Ciconia ciconia and Ciconia nigra*), white pelican (*Pelecanus onocrotalus*) and short-toed eagle (*Circaetus gallicus*), all heading south to winter quarters.

Winter is the time for the goose family from the north, especially in northern Bulgaria at Lake Shabla. Here you'll find healthy populations of the white-fronted, lesser white-fronted, red-breasted and greylag goose (*Anser albifrons, Anser erythropus, Branta ruficollis* and *Anser anser*).

Sreburna Reserve in northeastern Europe just south of the Danube has the largest colony of Dalmatian pelican (*Pelicanus crispus*) in Europe, at 220 pairs. There are just 20 pairs of imperial eagle (*Aquila heliaca*) but numerous glossy ibis (*Plegadis falcinellus*), booted eagle (*Hieraaetus pennatus*), and chukar (*Alectoris chukar*).

## Useful Organisations

Information and activities for bird watchers with affiliations to international organisations:

The Royal Society for the Protection of Birds (RSPB), The Lodge, Sandy, Beds, SG19 2DL, United Kingdom. *Tel: 01767 (+44 1767) 680551; www.rspb.org.uk*

Holidays for lovers of nature of all kinds, including bird watching trips, all run by a professional biologist:

Pandion D, 20A bul. Chemi Vrah, Sofia. *Tel/fax: (02) 963 0438. www.birdwatchingholidays.com.*

A useful book that is a mine of useful information on species and habitat is *Finding Birds in Bulgaria*, David Gosney (Gostours, 1993, ISBN 1898110026).

Facing page: Storks' nests are still common in many parts of Bulgaria
Below: The Burgas Lakes are a favourite area for bird watchers

# Shopping

Bulgaria has an exceptional range of arts and handicrafts that make excellent souvenirs. Prices range from very cheap for mass-produced items to thousands of pounds or dollars for unique pieces. The only difficulty you may have is in making a final choice and having enough room in your suitcase for all your purchases – watch your luggage allowance!

Traditional woodcarver

## What to buy

The two most widespread options are colourful patterned pottery, and lace and crocheted items hand-made by a veritable army of ladies, whose hands are at work even as they mind their stalls. Other interesting items are woven carpets and fabrics, carved wooden objects, icons, Russian dolls, jewellery made from shells, coral and semi-precious stones, wine, spirits, rose-scented foodstuffs and toiletries, art, antiques, communist and military memorabilia, and winter sports clothing and equipment.

## Where to buy
### SOFIA

For open-air shopping head to the collectors market in pl. Alexander Nevski, where you'll find old military souvenirs such as Russian medals, guns and swords. The alleyway between the square and the Military Club (on bul. Tsar Osvoboditel) is lined with stalls of art, while around the Alexander Nevski Church itself is the place to look at hand-made lace. The book market on bul. Slaveikov is an excellent place to browse for souvenir guides but also first

editions and second-hand editions in a range of languages. For general cheap and fun souvenirs try the underpass near the Sveta Petka Samardzhiiska Church and outside the Hali Market. Western-style shops and boutiques are making an impact. Try bul. Vitosha, or what was once communist Sofia's largest department store – the recently renovated TsUm on bul. Maria Luisa (*Tel: (02) 953 31 33*).

There are several shops and galleries where you can buy the highest quality handicrafts at commensurately high prices.

### Centre of Folk Arts and Crafts

Textiles, carpets, masks, icons, ceramics, jewellery, folk music, copies of museum pieces. Probably the best selection in Sofia.
*ul. Paris 4 and pl. Battenberg 2 (in the Ethnological Museum).*
*Tel: (02) 989 64 16;*
*www.bulgariancrafts.hit.bg.*

### The Icon Museum

Good quality modern icons. Many are copies of the originals in the museum.
*Crypt of Alexander Nevski Church, pl.*

*Alexander Nevski.*
*Tel: (02) 981 57 75.*

## Union of Bulgarian Artists

Range of traditional and modern styles
from a selection of Bulgaria's working
artists.
*bul. Vitosha 14.*
*Tel: (02) 946 71 13.*

## Carpet House

Traditional hand-woven kilims. You can
also have bespoke carpets woven with
your own design.
*ul. Rakovski 38 and 193.*
*Tel: (02) 983 66 09; www.tchukilim.com.*

## Traditzia

This non-profit making cooperative sells
a range of handicrafts from around
Bulgaria.
*bul. Vasil Levski 36.*
*Tel: (02) 981 77 65; www.traditizia.bg*

## CENTRAL BULGARIA
### Plovdiv

Plovdiv offers the largest range of
shopping in the region. The old town
has over 40 antique shops, many
congregated on ul. Saborna, where you
can pick up period lace, old
photographs, war memorabilia or
interesting communist-era items. All

Souvenir stalls, Sofia

Local cheap jewellery is fun to browse …

along ul. Saborna stalls sell traditional pottery, and artists use the railings to set up impromptu gallery space. More artists congregate around the Dzumaya Mosque – you'll get the full range from icons to abstract art. High street shopping is best on pedestrianised bul. Alexander Battenberg.

### Etur
Though it's not a huge complex, Etur has the full range of Bulgarian handicrafts, all fabricated by hand on site. You'll find a potter, weaver, leather-tooler, jeweller, woodcarver and icon painter within the complex. All are masters of their craft so prices are higher than for the mass-produced equivalent.
*7km southeast of Gabrovo.*
*Tel: (066) 801 830; www.etar.hit.bg.*

### Kotel
If you have a particular interest in carpets, head to Kotel, where they are still hand-made. Though there are no shops in town, the Carpet Exhibition Hall has a range on sale.
*ul. Izvorska 17.*
*Tel: (0453) 2316.*

### Koprivshtitsa and Tryavna
Koprivshtitsa is a little disappointing for shopping. There are a few souvenir shops and stalls around the main square selling lace and handicrafts. However, the streets of Tryavna have a good range of shops selling woodcarvings from simple bowls to ornate picture frames, pottery and locally produced art. This is a good place to browse.

### Oreshak
### The Exhibition of Applied Arts and Traditional Crafts Complex
A rather ugly modern building, but a repository for a comprehensive range of hand-made and mass-produced souvenirs.
*On the road to Troyan Monastery.*
*Tel: (0670) 22 062.*

### SOUTHWESTERN BULGARIA
Melnik is the place to buy wine. A host of shops and stalls sell locally produced labels along with local foodstuffs such as honey and jam. Treated sheepskins make excellent rugs.

The winter resorts of Pamporovo and Borovets offer competitive prices on winter sports equipment, especially at the end of the season. In summer an array of traditional lace and summer clothing takes the place of skis and poles.

Sadly the major monasteries don't have much in the way of good-quality souvenirs, concentrating mainly on mass-produced or lower-quality icons and religious items. You'll normally find a handful of souvenir stalls outside the gates – the largest selection sits outside Bachkovo.

### THE BLACK SEA COAST

The Stariyat Dobrich Complex is a good place to admire a range of Bulgarian handcrafted souvenirs and prices are reasonable. However, the choice doesn't come close to matching what you'd find on the streets of Nesebur, with its wealth of small galleries, pottery emporiums and little shops whose walls are swathed in lace, or to a lesser extent Sozopol.

At Balchik, an extensive crafts 'market' has set up stall on the approach to the Palace of Queen Marie – with some excellent traditional pottery, interesting jewellery and art. Prices are a little higher than elsewhere in the region because of the palace's popularity with tour groups.

There's a great collection of lace displayed outside the cathedral in Varna.

The major coastal resorts – Albena, Golden Sands, and Sunny Beach – all have a range of souvenir shops and stalls.

**Counterfeiters**
At Ladies' Market and the Book Market in Sofia (and in markets all across the country) you'll find counterfeit CDs and DVDs at a fraction of the cost of the genuine article. The prices may be tempting, but you've no guarantee that they'll play on your machine when you get home, and no guarantee of quality of the contents, indeed no guarantee that you'll actually get what's on the label.

... and there is always more serious jewellery shopping

# Icons

Icons are one of the most outstanding features of Orthodox Christian worship. Stylised depictions of Christ or of a venerated saint, they form the focus of worship because they are believed to be imbued with the Holy Spirit, and so are a direct conduit to heaven, with the ability to answer prayers and grant wishes. Believers pay homage to the icon, lighting candles to or even kissing the painting before making silent entreaties for strength, hope or courage in facing life's daily tribulations.

A number of icons are legendary, believed to be imbued with miraculous powers to save communities from famine, pestilence and war. They will normally be paraded through the streets on the saint's day at the head of a large procession, to bring luck to the population in the coming year. In addition to this, each saint has his or her own particular jurisdiction, acting as a spokesperson in the afterlife for farmers, fishermen, the sick or the infertile, for instance.

Icon painting began with the rise of the Eastern Christian or Byzantine Church at Constantinople after 330AD. The Orthodox form of Christianity spread north through the Balkans into Russia, southwest to Greece and southeast into Turkey and Syria as Byzantine religious influence and political power reached its zenith at around the time of the first millennium. Icon painting was the primary art form of Byzantium, a genre with complicated rules on form and style requiring use of the finest pure pigments, precious metals and even precious stones. But with the spread of Islam on the back of the expansion of the Ottoman Empire, icon painting became a clandestine activity concentrated in the monastery complexes.

## Creating an Icon

Traditional methods of creating an icon painting are time-consuming, requiring patience to work through the various processes and time to build up the layers of colour necessary to produce the finished results. Consequently, authentically painted modern icons are not cheap.

The painter starts with a panel of wood cut to the appropriate finished size, to which is fixed a fine cotton cloth or gauze, using rabbit skin glue, which is allowed to dry. He then heats rabbit skin glue with water and powder to make a gesso (a hard compound used as a base) and applies several thin coats of gesso over the cloth to build up a base. Each coat is allowed to dry before applying the next. Then the top layer is sanded with a fine glass paper for a smooth base.

The painter prepares a sketch of the final image on paper and draws an outline of this finished image on the panel. The panel is gilded by applying several layers of shellac (the resin of the lac insect) on top of which is added a layer of mixion (gold glue) and 23-carat gold leaf.

Painting can now begin. A tempera (water mixed with egg yolk and vinegar) is mixed as a base. This will be combined with various natural minerals to create the vivid colours. These paints are applied in numerous thin layers to create depth of colour. The halo of gold leaf is the last to be applied. In Bulgarian icon painting the halo traditionally has an embossed profile and this is achieved by applying natural resins to the surface. The icon is left for many weeks for the colours to settle before the final varnish is applied.

## Icon Studio

This studio produces hand-painted icons in the traditional way. Prices start at around 70 leva for a 10 x 5cm icon. Bespoke icons of any size can be ordered and will be shipped.
*Rossen Donchev, Etur Tel: GSM 0887 108333; www.art.edebag.com*

Facing page: traditional methods of icon painting are slow and painstaking
Left: though the genuine article is not cheap, a hand-painted icon makes a wonderful souvenir of Bulgaria

# Entertainment

The arts were well subsidised under the communist regime. Ticket prices were low and even relatively small towns had viable theatre companies. Today the subsidies have gone and ticket prices have had to be raised (though prices are still cheap by western standards) and consequently audiences for the mainstream arts have fallen. This, combined with the fact that the younger generation now look to western pop culture, has caused the closure of some companies outside the capital.

Concert poster

That said, there are still centres of excellence and many worthwhile performances if you enjoy the classical arts. Sofia is the obvious high spot. It has an excellent and varied programme of exhibitions, along with respected opera, ballet and orchestral companies. But others include Plovdiv, Varna and Ruse, where you'll also find one or more experienced ballet, opera, theatre or orchestral companies. Bulgaria's numerous festivals include classical and arts performances, often in atmospheric outdoor venues such as parks or Roman amphitheatres.

As the classical arts have declined from their peak under communism, other forms of entertainment have taken their place in the major cities and summer and winter resorts. Cinema, bars and club/discos are popular and you'll find a thriving gambling scene with numerous casinos, often linked to the major hotels, especially along the Black Sea coast.

Out in the countryside it's a total contrast to the resorts and the capital.

Some provincial towns will have music bars or a cinema but otherwise your entertainment is confined to dinner and an early night.

The fount of all wisdom for entertainment is the *Sofia Echo* (*www.sophiaecho.com*), which provides up-to-date information on activities for the week ahead in its supplement with ticketing and timing information in English. It's published every Friday and is available in hotels and at newsstands. *Sofia Inside and Out* is published seasonally and has a section on Culture and Leisure. It's available free at most hotels.

## Classical Performance Venues

Bulgaria has several impressive late 19th-century opera/theatre venues that play host to both their own and touring companies. Sofia sees many international orchestral and opera companies. Be aware that many domestic companies take a break in the summer and venues may close completely during August.

## SOFIA
### National Opera House
Home of the National Opera Company, and venue for touring companies. Full opera programme.
*ul. Vrabcha 1. Tel: (02) 981 15 49.*

### Stefan Makedonski Theatre
Light operetta and musicals.
*pl. Battenberg 1. Tel: (02) 944 23 21.*

## RUSE
### Ruse Opera
Hosts professional and amateur performances.
*pl. Sveta Troitsa 7. Tel: (082) 225 368. Ticket office at ul. Alexandrovska 61. Tel: (082) 234 303.*

## PLOVDIV
### National Opera House
Opera and philharmonic performances.
*pl. Tsentralen 1. Tel: (032) 63 22 31.*

### Plovdiv Drama Theatre
Also called the Nikolai Masalitinov Drama Theatre. Stages mainly European classical performances including Shakespeare – however, performances are in Bulgarian (which could give *Romeo and Juliet* or *King Lear* a new twist if you already know the plot!)
*ul. Knyaz Alexander Battenberg 38. Tel: (032) 632 348.*

## STARA ZAGORA
### Stara Zagora Opera
Visiting companies play here throughout the season (Oct–May).
*bul. Tsar Simeon Veliki 108. Tel: (042) 224 81.*

## VARNA
### Varna Opera
The most important house after Sofia, with a resident company.
*pl. Nezavisimost. Tel: (052) 22 25 44.*

Varna Opera House

## Concerts

The classical concert programme is full and varied, with Bulgarian and international artists filling halls large and small. Popular and modern music concerts tend to be limited to the capital. More and more international artists are adding Sofia to their itinerary – though tickets sell out fast for the legends of rock and pop. Here are some major venues:

### SOFIA
#### NDK National Palace of Culture

Fifteen different-sized halls for performances of all kinds. This is normally the venue where international pop acts appear when they visit Bulgaria.
*pl. Bulgaria 1. Tel: (02) 916 23 00.*

#### Bulgaria Hall

Home to the Sofia Philharmonic orchestra, with a large hall and a smaller chamber hall.

*ul. Aksakov 1. Tel: (ticket office) (02) 987 76 56.*

#### Slaveikov Hall

A range of classical recitals and concerts.
*pl. Slaveikov 3. Tel: (02) 988 23 49.*

#### National Musical Theatre

Usually holds performances in Bulgarian.
*bul. Vasil Levski 100. Tel: (02) 943 19 79.*

### VARNA
#### Festival and Congress Hall

Several function halls for concerts and presentations.
*bul. Slivnitsa 2. Tel: (052) 213 31; www.fcclhit.bg.*

#### Open-air Theatre, Primorski Park

Often a venue in the summer arts festival for theatre performances and live music.
*Tel: (052) 228 385.*

Dance performance

**Palais de Culture (Festival Hall)**
Hosts events for all Varna's festivals (the summer festival runs throughout the summer with concerts) and competitions. It also plays host to the Varna Film Festival in early September.
*bul. Tsar Boris I 115. Tel: (052) 228 019.*

**Theatre Varnenska Komouna**
*pl. Metropolite Simeon 1.*
*Tel: (052) 222 042.*

**PLOVDIV**
**Marionettes Theatre**
Bulgarian Puppet Theatre.
*bul. Hristo Danov 14. Tel: (032) 631 147.*

**Roman Theatre**
Renovated Roman Theatre used during the summer for concerts and other special events.
*ul. Hemus.*

**ALBENA**
**Albena Variety Theatre**
Shows and spectacles throughout the summer.
*Albena Cultural Centre.*
*Tel: (057) 962 251.*

**Cultural Institutes**
Sofia has several cultural institutes. These hold regular exhibitions and concerts promoting their own national artists, plus regular social gatherings to promote cross-cultural understanding.

**SOFIA**
**British Council**
*ul. Krakra 7. Tel: (02) 942 43 44.*

**Euro-Bulgarian Cultural Institute**
*bul. Stamboliiski 17. Tel: (02) 988 00 84.*

**French Cultural Gallery**
*bul. Vasil Levski 2. Tel: (02) 981 69 27.*

**Italian Cultural Institute**
*ul. Alexander Zhendov 1.*
*Tel: (02) 971 47 98.*

**Arts, Folk and Cultural Events**
Traditional music, song and dance together form one of the strongest elements of Bulgaria's collective cultural identity. You'll see these in some form at every domestic festival.

Bulgaria has so many cultural events that the Festivals and Events section (*see pp24–5*) barely scratches the surface.

Included here are a number of additional major arts festivals that add cultural richness throughout the year.
**February** The Albert Roussel International Piano Concourse, Sofia
**April** Man and Earth Festival, Sofia
**May** Sofia Musical Weeks, Sofia
**June** International Contemporary Music Festival, Sofia
**July** Festival of Tzigane (Gypsy) Music, Stara Zagora
**August** Vitosha Folklore Festival, Sofia
**September** International Theatre Festival, Burgas

It's always worth asking your hotel concierge or holiday rep about local festivals taking place during your stay. Even the smallest village has a couple of celebrations each year, and this is definitely one way to see Bulgarians having fun.

## Cinema

All major towns have cinema houses or multiscreen complexes. Films are shown in the original language with Cyrillic subtitles, so provided you can ignore the stream of print at the bottom of the screen, it's easy to enjoy the latest Hollywood blockbusters in English.

### SOFIA
**Theatre Moderne**
*bul. Maria Luisa 26. Tel: (02) 983 56 46.*

**Multiplex**
*NPK, pl. Bulgaria 1. Tel: (02) 951 51 01.*

**FX Cinema**
*ul. Angel Kanchev 5. Tel: (02) 981 27 17.*

**Levski Cinema**
*bul. Yanko Sakazov 28. Tel: (02) 846 71 71.*

**Serdika**
*pl. Vasil Levski. Tel: (02) 843 17 97.*

### PLOVDIV
**Europa Cinema**
*Plovdiv Fairground. Tel: (032) 61 35.*

**Flamingo Cinema**
*bul. 6 Sevtembri 128. Tel: (032) 432 032.*

**Lucky Cinema**
*ul. Gladstone 1. Tel: (032) 629 070.*

## Galleries

Commercial galleries have grown in importance in the post-communist Bulgaria. These represent up and coming Bulgarian artists but also have collections from abroad.

### SOFIA
**Art-Is Gallery**
*bul. Gurko 14. Tel: (02) 986 72 61.*

**Cyclops Gallery**
*ul. Krum Popov 79. Tel: (02) 963 49 44.*

**Festinvest Gallery**
*bul. Tsar Assen II 26. Tel: (02) 943 48 11.*

## Bars, Clubbing and Discotheques

Discos and clubs are popular in the big cities. However, this sector is particularly prone to change, with clubs opening up and going out of business within a season. All the large hotels offer a music venue of some kind. They are your best options in the coastal resorts and the capital. The establishments mentioned here are all successful and long-standing venues.

### SOFIA
**Biblioteka Disco**
The place to meet the Sofia in crowd.
*bul. Vasil Levski 88. Tel: (02) 943 40 04.*
*Open: nightly 8.30pm. Admission charge.*

**Nai Club**
Eclectic live music venue, disco and folk venue with DJs several nights a week.
*pl. Narodno Sabranie 10.*
*Tel: (02) 981 27 47. Open 7pm–5am.*
*Admission charge.*

**Piano Bar Jack**
Live piano music nightly.
*ul. Rakovski 98. Tel: (02) 987 91 98.*

**JJ Murphy's**
Irish bar with live music at weekends.
*ul. Karnigradska 7. Tel: (02) 980 28 70.*

**Club Latino Caramba**
Latin music and Latin food.
*At the Hotel Bulgaria, bul. Tsar
Osvoboditel 4. Tel: (02) 987 07 78.*

**Chervilo**
Young and trendy clientele.
*bul. Tsar Osvoboditel 9. Tel: (02) 981
6633; www.chervilo.com.*

**Artists Bar**
Live piano music Mon–Tue, jazz
Wed–Thur.
*Hilton Hotel. Tel: (02) 993 50 00.*

**Motto**
Trendy restaurant/bar with live music
Thur–Sat.
*ul. Aksakov 18. Tel: (02) 987 27 23.*

**HISAR**
**Coliseum Nightclub**
*bul. Ivan Vazov 18. Tel: (087) 293 503.
Open: daily 10pm–6am.*

**PLOVDIV**
**Club Santo**
Complex of restaurant, folk bar and
disco.
*bul. Maritza 122.
Tel: (032) 627 171.*

**Club Plazma**
Newest club in the city, concentrating
on house music.
*Stochna Gara. Tel: 887 572 825.*

**Club Neolit**
Hosts different music evenings from
retro to garage.
*bul. Hristo Botev 51.
Tel: 888 817 555.*

**Sky Bar**
Plays whatever's popular at the time.
*ul. Knyaz Battenberg. Tel: (032) 633 777.*

**VARNA**
**Disco Danvi**
Under the Opera House and popular
with the young hip crowd.
*pl. Nezavisimost. No phone.*

**Casinos**
Gambling in the grand traditional
manner has gone hand in hand with the
spa resorts since the mid 18th century.
It's a popular pastime with Bulgarians
and today you'll find a number of
casinos in the capital and on the Black
Sea where the tables are open to all
comers. Just don't lose your shirt!

**SOFIA**
**Hotel Hemus**
*bul. Cherni Vrah 31. Tel: (02) 963 55 66.*

**Hotel Princess**
*bul. Maria Luisa 131. Tel: (02) 933 87 00.*

**SVETI KONSTANTIN**
**Grand Hotel Varna**
*Tel: (052) 357 182.*

**PLOVDIV**
**Hotel Trimontium Princess**
*pl. Tsentralen. Tel: (032) 605 000.*

**VARNA**
**Casino International**
*ul. Zolotye Peski. Tel: (052) 357 194.*

**SUNNY BEACH**
**Balkan Tourist Hotel**
*Tel: (0554) 27 59.*

# Children

Bulgaria is not particularly set up for children but that is not to say it's not child-friendly. It's more perhaps that because children are freer to play in the old-fashioned sense than they are now in the West they are often left to make their own entertainment. The attitude to children is positive. They stay out late, are welcomed at restaurants and boisterous behaviour is generally indulged rather than frowned upon.

Enjoying a ride

Though there are few specific attractions for children, Bulgaria has some advantages. The town and city centres will usually have a core of traffic-free streets where you won't need to keep your kids glued to your side for fear of their getting run over. Most towns and cities have areas of parkland and shady squares where kids can let off steam. Most parks have a small collection of child-sized battery-powered coin-operated cars and trucks but few have swings and slides. Popcorn and candyfloss sellers cater to even the largest appetites.

## Where for Kids
### The Black Sea

The Black Sea resorts are by far the most child-friendly areas for activities. Of course the beaches keep children of all ages happy throughout the day but top that with a good range of watersports, small funfairs at each of the resorts, a couple of bowling alleys and karting tracks for older kids and you have something for the whole family. Most three-star hotels and above have decent-

sized pools and four-star hotels normally offer communal entertainment, though dedicated 'kid's clubs' are not common (you will find them at the Hotel Pomorie at Sunny Beach and the Hotel Sirene at Golden Sands).

There's always something to fill the evenings in every resort. The streets are lined with shops and stalls offering face painting, temporary henna tattoos and hair braiding, or old fairground-style games of chance. There's even the opportunity to have your picture taken in Victorian or other historical costume.

### Sofia

Sofia would seem to have little to offer children. The most 'fun' museum is the Natural History Museum, with its collection of stuffed animals. But South Park (Simeonovsko Shosse) in the south of the city has a selection of sporting and other attractions including tennis courts and swimming pools (though these get very busy, especially in summer). There's also a small zoo with exotic animals including lions, tigers and elephants. Few hotels in the capital have a swimming pool, as most cater primarily for business clients. The Hotel Princess in Sofia is the only one with a dedicated children's pool.

## What for Kids
### Festivities and Saint's Days

There's always a festival going on somewhere in Bulgaria and there's nothing that children love more than a parade, be it merry or sombre. Folk dancing in traditional costume is a major form of cultural expression and as Bulgarian children are enthusiastic members of dance troupes this enthusiasm is bound to rub off on visiting children. There's always an associated fair with rides, market stalls, and snacks. There should be enough going on to fill the whole day.

### Skiing and snowboarding

The majority of ski runs in Bulgarian resorts are greens and blues, perfect for young children just starting out. Packages to Bulgaria are good value, making it the perfect place for a first time trip or a taster holiday.

Children's entertainment in Bulgaria is based on simple fun more than purpose-built attractions

# Sport and Leisure

## SPECTATOR SPORTS

Bulgaria has a couple of organised sports that visitors may want to see, though this is one area of life that has suffered greatly since the well-funded programmes of the communist era ended.

## Football (Soccer)

Like much of the world Bulgarians take their football much more seriously than their politics. Their league is not one of the strongest in Europe but their two most successful teams are the Sofia-based CSKA (*www.cska.bg*) and Levski (*www.levski.bg*). Both have made several forays into European competition.

## Alpine and Cross-Country Winter Events

Bulgaria has played host to a handful of alpine skiing races, with Borovets being the most important venue. To see if it's on the calendar during any particular season consult the Federation International du Ski (FIS) (*www.fis-ski.com*).

Levski Sofia's home ground

## PARTICIPATION SPORTS AND LEISURE ACTIVITIES

Bulgaria is beginning to develop its leisure activity provision as tourism grows in importance but is somewhat limited by a lack of modern equipment, few places to hire equipment and few competent English-speaking instructors. However, for sports people already experienced it offers new and exciting playgrounds for some activities and two of its major strengths in leisure activities (bird watching and hiking) require no technical expertise at all.

The following organisations specialise in a full range of sporting and activity tours/holidays in Bulgaria and can help you plan and book a trip:

**Zig Zag Holidays**
*bul. Stamboliiski 20v, Sofia 1000.*
*Tel: (02) 980 51 02; www.zigzag.dir.bg*
**Odysseia-In Sport and Travel Agency**
*bul. Stamboliiski 20a, Sofia 1000.*
*Tel: (02) 989 05 38; www.odysseia-in.com*

### Bird Watching

With hectares of pristine countryside and a vast range of divergent natural habitats, Bulgaria offers abundant opportunity for twitchers. Over 350 species call the place home or pass through on regular migratory journeys, stopping for a few days to re-energise, and the country has several internationally important protected areas with over 150 species regularly on view (*see pp142–3*).

### Canoeing and Kayaking

With myriad freshwater lakes, and well-developed river systems to enjoy, it is no surprise that canoeing and kayaking are

Bulgaria is one of Europe's best destinations for bird watching

popular activities here, particularly in the spring when water levels are high with the melt water from the mountain snows. However, equipment hire isn't widespread and it's not always so easy to find competent tuition in English if you are a beginner. Several of the restaurants on the banks of Lake Iskur rent out kayaks and pedalos by the hour or day.

Make sure that you have life jackets – particularly for children.

### Hiking

Bulgaria is an exceptional destination for hikers. With outstanding scenery, well-marked footpaths and a network of mountain huts offering simple accommodation it's possible to extend hikes over hundreds of kilometres and

There are many opportunities for family-sized short hikes

to spend weeks en route, a complete alternative to the Sofia city break or Black Sea beach type of holiday.

Numerous short day-hikes of between 1 and 20 kilometres can be found in the Vitosha National Park just south of Sofia, the Rila Mountains in the southwest, Pirin Mountains in the Rodopi Mountains and the central Stara Planina range. For more on national parks, *see pp134–41*. You can pick a route to suit your pace and fitness level; all you require is sturdy footwear and appropriate clothing for the weather conditions.

Trails are marked by coloured signs that correspond to plotted routes on good maps (*see box*). These are easy to follow requiring no specialist navigation skills.

The Bulgarian Association for

Rural & Ecological Travel (BARET) is responsible for instigating a number of ecotrails either through some of Bulgaria's most notable countryside or incorporating its most famous monuments. These include a route from Dryanovo Monastery and one in Vrachanska Balkan National Park.

Bulgaria has over 300 mountain huts on longer-distance and more challenging routes offering basic overnight accommodation, warm food and sanitary facilities. For details about booking huts *tel: (02) 980 1285*.

**Hiking Maps**
Domino (*www.domino.bg*) produce a range of maps of the various National Parks showing the walking and hiking routes, though they are printed in Cyrillic. The best range of these is available at the book market on bul. Graf Ignatiev in Sofia.

## Horse Riding

The slow pace of trekking on horseback is excellent for wandering through the Bulgarian countryside and is becoming an increasingly popular option at the major tourist hotspots. For those with no experience, however, there are few places to get lessons in English.

The forests of Borovets offer excellent trails in the summer (hired from the Hotel Rila or contact Butch Rider, *tel: 087 660 119*). Pamporovo also has provision in summer – choose from a selection waiting around the central junction of the town. Other locations with a more organised set-up are the Arbanasi Horse Base (*Tel: (062) 36 68*) in Arbanasi in central Bulgaria, and the Tourist Centre at Sozopol (*Tel: (088) 853 29 76*) and Kona Bazza Riding School (*Tel: (048) 776 056*) at Albena, both on the Black Sea coast.

## Mountain Biking

Increasingly popular along the hiking routes all across Bulgaria, mountain biking is limited at the moment because of a lack of places to rent equipment. The easiest places are at the ski resorts, where the winter pistes become summer trails and you can rent equipment at Mount Vitosha, Borovets and Pamporovo.

Mountain biking is particularly easy in the Stara Planina, where tourist offices affiliated with the Association

### Insurance

Some of the sports and activities suggested here may not be covered by a standard travel insurance policy. Always check with your insurance company that you are covered before heading out to Bulgaria or, alternatively, check that the company you are organising the activity with has liability cover in the event of an accident.

The quiet Bulgarian countryside is ideal for riding

The Black Sea coast is well developed for watersports

Stara Planina hire bikes by the hour or day – and gradients aren't as steep as on Vitosha.

A new initiative with Swiss assistance has designated a series of mountain bike tracks around Troyan, Gabrovo and Teteven with rides of different lengths and ability levels, linking major tourist attractions to form a tour of several days. Maps will be available at tourist offices in each of the towns. You can also rent a bike and a guide if you want one.

**Mountaineering and Climbing**
Bulgaria's mountains make an excellent playground for the experienced climber. The birthplace of the sport, the Iskur Gorge, is still popular, while Maliovitsa in the Rila Mountains is a centre of excellence, with several alpine peaks close by. The serrated surfaces of White

Rocks National Park attract free climbers and mountaineers for their short testing ascents, while several of the peaks over 2,000m offer reasonable challenges for a more organised expedition.

The Bulgarian Alpine Club (*bul. Vasil Levski 75, Sofia. Tel: (02) 930 0532; www.bac.netbg.com*) can offer information and help with arranging climbs.

**Potholing and Spelunking**
Blessed with some exceptionally fine cave systems – over 4000 documented caverns and potholes, the longest being over 15km long, the deepest at 415m – Bulgaria offers challenges for even the most experienced caver. The best sites are in the karst regions west of Vratsa, in the western Rodopi Mountains and the Pirin karst.

Beginners are not well catered for and are advised to enjoy the guided tours of some of the larger cave complexes mentioned in the What to See section of this guide rather than head underground alone.

Club Extreme (*www.clubextreme.org*) offers tours. No training is provided, only guided trips – therefore unsuitable for beginners.

### Scuba Diving

Not as widespread along the Black Sea coast as one might expect, so Bulgaria might not be the place to get your initial certification; there are few instructors in English and few places to hire equipment if you already have certification. This situation should improve over the next few years.

### Skiing
*See pp100–101.*

### Spas and Therapeutic Treatments
*See next page.*

### Watersports
When it comes to watersports Albena is the nation's capital. This purpose-built resort offers everything that the enthusiast of any age would want, from banana boat rides to water skiing, windsurfing and jet skiing. Numerous kiosks on the beachfront offer equipment rental but not instruction.

Watersports, but not necessarily the whole range, are also available at Golden Sands, Sunny Beach, Sozopol, Pomorie, Primorsko and Dyuni along the Black Sea.

Windsurfing on Lake Iskur

Wellbeing is the mantra of the new millennium, an era when a little pampering seems to have transcended the barrier from luxury item to human right. Today, the spa is the place to be seen enjoying a plethora of non-invasive cosmetic procedures. If you are looking for somewhere different to spend a little down time, try Bulgaria.

The country has an exceptional wealth of natural mineral springs, hot springs and beneficial mud that have been the basis of treatments for centuries. The Greeks and particularly the Romans had a love of bathing – it was almost as much about socialising as cleanliness. Some of the most renowned spas in the Roman Empire were in Bulgaria at Hisar, Sandanski, Sliven and Burgas – these were further developed as the Roman Empire gave way to the Byzantine.

During Ottoman rule, the Islamic precept of cleanliness drove further development of huge baths complexes open to all and the newly independent Bulgaria was inaugurated at about the same time as Victorian Europe discovered complementary medicines. Doctors would happily prescribe a sojourn in the mountains and on the coast as a treatment for a range of conditions. Grand spas such as that at Sveti Konstantin in Bulgaria were filled with guests from royalty to the new glitterati – writers, composers and playwrights.

Though Westerners disappeared from the spas of Bulgaria during the communist era, Russians took their places in vast numbers. The population became used to being prescribed complementary therapies as part of an underfunded and non-innovative health service, so much so that they were regarded as mainstream treatments for skin disorders, high blood pressure, breathing problems, arthritis, nervous

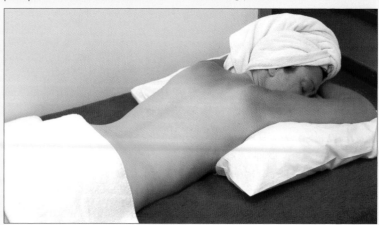

conditions and kidney and liver complaints.

Today there are over 500 balneotherapy centres in Bulgaria and 250 thermal sources. Each offers a different speciality and some only deal with medical cases. The most developed pleasure spas can be found on the Black Sea coast at Albena, Sunny Beach, Golden Sands and Sveti Konstantin. A useful source of information is the Bulgarian Balneology Association (*Bul. Javorov 40, 8200 Pomorie. Tel: (0596) 5866; www.bab-bg.org*).

The town with the largest number of mineral springs in Bulgaria is Velingrad, with over 70. The hottest spring is the one in Sapereva Banya near Dupnitsa, with a constant temperature of 40°C. It is claimed to be the hottest in Europe.

## A Quick Guide to Spa Treatments

**Aromatherapy** – use of essential oils to improve mood or ameliorate minor conditions.

**Detox or detoxification** – the process of removing toxins – substances that are damaging or poisonous, such as coffee or alcohol, from the body.

**Exfoliation** – removal of the upper layers of the epidermis to eliminate toxins and promote new skin growth.

**Helio-prophylaxis** – sunlight therapy.

**Inhalations** – for lung problems and for re-oxygenation of the system.

**Mud treatments** – infuse minerals into or leach toxins out of the skin.

**Ozone and oxygen therapy** – like an ozone 'sauna' to eliminate free radicals.

**Reflexology** – the belief that areas of the feet are linked to areas of the body. Massage of these points promotes improvement in problem areas of the body.

**Seaweed wrap** – the body is coated in seaweed extract to re-mineralise and re-hydrate the skin.

**Thalassotherapy** – use of seawater for massage.

Although spas were operated as part of the health service under the communist regime, the accent of today's treatments is the body beautiful

# Food and Drink

Eating out in Bulgaria can be a pleasure. Food is delicious and cheap (bearing in mind the caveat Tourists Beware, *see box opposite*) though the impenetrable barrier to foreigners, the Cyrillic language, still presents some problems with menus. But don't let a small challenge with language spoil your exploration of Bulgarian cuisine.

Restaurant sign

## Where to Eat

You'll find a range of eateries available in Bulgaria. The self-service cafeteria allows you to point at what you want rather than having to work your way through the menu. Cafeterias also offer excellent value and tasty fare. A *mehana* is a Bulgarian tavern where waiters wear traditional costumes. Restaurants range from informal to formal with prices from inexpensive to exorbitant.

## What to Eat

### Bulgarian Dishes

Bulgarian cuisine has influences from both Greece and Turkey and comprises a range of delicious summer and winter dishes. In winter Bulgarians start with a hearty soup, perhaps *bob* (bean soup) or *topcheta supa* (soup with meatballs). In summer, salad is favoured, normally the *shopska salata* (tomatoes, cucumber and onion topped with grated cheese), which can be found just about everywhere. A small range of starter dishes or dips can also be ordered including *tarator* (yoghurt soup with cucumber and walnuts), *mletcha salata* (yoghurt with cucumber, walnuts and garlic), *sarmi* (vine or cabbage leaves stuffed with rice and spices, sometimes

with meat) or *kashkaval pane* (breaded fried cheese).

The basis of most main courses is simple grilled meats – chops, ribs and steaks. *Meshana skara*, the Bulgarian equivalent of a mixed grill, is a popular choice. Other items include *kebabche*, a grilled spicy sausage, and *kyufke*, a spicy meat patty.

Bulgarians also have a delicious range of slow-cooked dishes, including its national dish *kavarma* (a slowly cooked stew of pork and liver), *drob sarma* (chopped liver, rice and eggs baked in the oven) and *sirene po shopski* (eggs and cheese baked in a clay pot with tomatoes). *Musaka* could be mistaken for the Greek moussaka but doesn't contain aubergine. If you work out the word *gyuvech* on the menu you'll be ordering meat stew.

Fish is popular along the Black Sea coast but will always be more expensive than meat. *Plakiya* is a delicious fish stew with no written

### Side Dishes

You must order all side dishes (bread, vegetables, potatoes) separately to your meat, chicken or fish and there will be a charge for each item.

recipe – just made with whatever was caught that day.

Bulgarians like to start the day with a *banitsa*, a warm pastry filled with cheese.

## International Cuisine

The large five-star hotels generally have a high-class restaurant serving international and continental cuisine at high prices. Chinese restaurants are numerous, along with Italian restaurants and pizzerias.

At the other end of the scale the international fast food chains have certainly made their presence felt, while the Bulgarian chain Happy Bar and Grill serve good value Western-style dishes.

## Drinks

Although drinking water is said to be safe, bottled water will certainly taste better. The short shot of strong coffee (espresso style) oils the wheels of Bulgarian society; it is available everywhere and is excellent. For tea,

Bulgarians drink *bilkov* (herbal) or *plodov* (fruit) teas. Fresh fruit juices are a highlight of the summer, while the international brands of pop (soda) are readily available.

Bulgarian wine (*see pp170–71*) is well regarded. The country also brews good beer; leading brands include Kamenitsa and Zagorka. For something with more oomph, try domestic brands of vodka, excellent *slivova rakiya* (plum brandy) and *rosaliika* (rose liqueur). International liquor favourites are available but at a price premium.

Useful phrase – *Na Zdrave* means 'Cheers'.

> **Tourists Bewate**
> Overcharging is not uncommon, especially at Black Sea coastal resorts and in winter resorts. Don't order from a menu without prices indicated on it. Try to get a menu in Cyrillic and English as these should show the true 'normal' price. Always check your final bill.

Bulgarian food has a strong affinity with Greek and Turkish cuisine

## Restaurants

In the selection below, restaurants have been marked according to price levels, on the basis of prices for a three-course meal for one without wine:

★ Under 8 leva
★★ 8–12 leva
★★★ 13–16 leva
★★★★ Over 16 leva

### SOFIA

**Vkusnata Skara ★★**
One of the most popular cafeterias in the city and close to all the attractions. The food is simple but delicious and the portions are large.
*bul. Stamboliiski 33.*
*Tel: (02) 453 16 36.*

**Beyond the Alley, Behind the Cupboard ★★★**
Long-standing restaurant set in a renovated late 19th-century mansion. International menu.
*ul. Budapest 31.*
*Tel: (02) 983 55 88.*

**Flannagans ★★★★**
A magnet for ex-pats, Flannagans is an Irish-style bar serving American fast food and English pub grub.
*pl. Narodno Sabrinie.*
*Tel: (02) 986 79 83.*

**Pizza Victoria ★★★**
Very popular pizzeria, though there's plenty more on the menu. Good food and pleasant terrace for summer eating.
*Rear of the Military Club, bul. Tsar Osvoboditel.*
*Tel: (02) 943 75 43.*

### CENTRAL BULGARIA

**Tryavna**
**Starata Loza ★★**
This charming restaurant in the old town serves a combination of Bulgarian and continental dishes.
*ul. Slaveikov 44.*
*Tel: (0677) 45 01.*

**Veliko Turnovo**
**Starata Mehana ★**
Tiny restaurant with simple but well-cooked Bulgarian fare and great views over the town. Menu in English.
*ul. Fitcheto 3.*
*Tel: (062) 436 13.*

**Koprivshtitsa**
**Chuchura ★★**
Traditional Bulgarian restaurant set by the river with quality food and a good atmosphere.
*ul. Palaveev 66.*
*Tel: (07184) 27 12.*

**Etur**
**Mehana Renaissance ★★**
Set on the bank of a stream, this *mehana* serves good Bulgarian food during museum opening hours.
*Museum Complex.*
*Tel: 801 691.*

**Hisar**
**National Garden Restaurant ★★**
Good Bulgarian food in a pretty courtyard garden setting.
*Rabotno Vreme, ul. Gurko.*
*Tel: (0337) 25 80.*

The familiar kebab is a Bulgarian staple

## SOUTHWEST BULGARIA

### Bansko

**Motikata ★★★**
Famed throughout the region for its barbecued meats, which you can enjoy in summer in the large garden with stunning views of the mountains.
*On the road from the town to the ski slopes.*
*Tel: (07443) 82 49.*

Traditionally rustic restaurant decor

### Melnik

**Hotel Dospat Slav ★★★★**
Fine continental cuisine at a reasonable price in a dining room furnished in wrought iron.
*No street address.*
*Tel: (07437) 271.*

### Plovdiv

**Alafrangite ★★★★**
High-class restaurant serving almost nouvelle cuisine style food. One of a handful of more Western-style restaurants in the city.
*ul. Kiril Nectariev 17.*
*Tel: (032) 269 595.*

## BLACK SEA COAST

### Burgas

**Marakas ★★**
This café/bar decorated in Art Deco style is the in place in town. Snacks, salads and full meals are served throughout the day.
*ul. Bogoridi. No phone.*

### Nesebur

**Kapitanska Sreshta ★★★★**
The best seafood restaurant along the southern coast always has a fresh selection of fish, lobster and imported Russian caviar. If you like fish you'll want to splash out here.
*ul. Mena.*
*Tel: (0554) 421 24.*

### Varna

**Chuchurite ★★**
Lovely dining room with Bulgarian carpets and soft furnishings. Specialities of meats cooked on an open grill. Menu in English.
*ul. Panagiuriste 15.*
*Tel: (052) 637 117.*

### Balchik

**Korona ★★★**
Good place for lunch. Specialises in fresh seafood.
*On the beach in front of the palace.*
*Tel: (0579) 759 18.*

## THE NORTH

### Ruse

**Pizza Roma ★**
Popular pizzeria serving a range of other Italian dishes. Photo menu helps in your choice.
*ul. Maria Louisa 2.*
*Tel: (082) 257 57.*

### Vidin

**Cappello ★**
Lively bar/restaurant with pizzas and pasta on the menu. Good value for money.
*ul. Tsar Alexander II.*
*Tel: (094) 372 97.*

Bulgarian wine production started late. The Romans didn't seem to see the benefit of the country's fine soil, preferring warmer climates such as Greece and southern Italy for their vineyards. It was only as Rome gave way to Byzantium in the 6th century that vines were planted in the area around Melnik, but the Bulgars learned fast.

Not all of the country is suitable for wine production, but Bulgaria's deep mountain valleys, its very varied soil types and its combination of weather systems combine to produce several excellent micro-climates.

Much of the production was given over to domestic consumption until the communist era, when a successful export market grew quickly in the years after the 1960s. Before the fall of the regime the country was in the top 10 wine exporters. Much of it arrived in UK off-licences. Bulgaria became renowned for its cheap hearty red *vin de table*, the staple reliable budget choice for millions of Brits.

Unfortunately, with the fall of the regime, the wine industry suffered the same problems as many Bulgarian industries – market forces didn't sit well on the newly independent managements' shoulders and exports dropped. The wine market was also changing and drinkers were demanding higher quality than Bulgarian producers could supply in the short term.

The most forward-thinking began a process of reinvestment, replanting old and more rustic domestic varieties of vine with internationally recognised varieties such as Merlot and Chardonnay.

In 2002, 57 million litres of bottled wine were exported. Bulgaria was 17th in the world for area under vines and the country had more than 50 wineries. The best are producing some well-respected wine, though there are still many quaffable, less expensive options to explore.

## Quality of Wine

There are several levels of quality for Bulgarian wine.

The basic quality is table wine. This is always a blend of unspecified grape varieties and does not denote the origin of the wine.

Country wine is another blend, but

this time only two grape varieties can be combined and these must be stated on the label.

Wines of Declared Geographical Origin (DGO) are made from a single grape variety within a specific geographical location. At present these constitute 70% of Bulgarian production.

Controlled Appellation of Origin (AOC) wines are classified in line with the French system of quality control. They have to be made of a specific grape variety in vineyards with specific yield limits per hectare within a denoted region.

DGO and AOC wines achieve reserve status if they have been aged in oak for more than three years for reds or two years for whites.

## Grape Varieties

For reds, the French grape varieties Merlot and Cabernet Sauvignon are being planted but local red varieties include: Gamza, the most widespread grape, producing soft, fruity, light-bodied wine; Mavrud, producing full-bodied red that ages well; Melnik, mostly grown in the southeast, producing heavy reds that age well; and Pamid, the mainstay of much of the table wine.

Whites made from international grape varieties such as Chardonnay, Sauvignon Blanc and Riesling are available, but you may also find local varieties Misket, Ottonel and Diamat.

## Labels to Look For

The following wineries/regions have a high reputation:
Damiantza
Vini Sliven
Suhindol
Domaine Boyar
Slavyantsi
Haskovo
St Nikola

## Wine Tours

Romantic Wine Tours (*ul. Buzladju 47, Sofia; tel: (02) 9516466, fax: (02) 9515272; www.romaticwinetours.com*) offers escorted wine tours around Bulgaria for individuals and groups.

Facing page: Bulgarian winemakers are steadily improving quality for the export market
Below: The wines of Melnik are highly regarded

# Hotels and Accommodation

Bulgaria has a wide range of accommodation possibilities, though there is a great difference in provision between town and country. Five-star hotels are few and concentrated in the capital but there is more provision at the four- and three-star level in the major towns and cities, and of course along the Black Sea coast, with concentrations at Albena, Sunny Beach and Golden Sands.

Sheraton Sofia Hotel Balkan

Beyond the major tourist centres prices really drop, but most hotels fall into the three- and two-star categories. Many so-called hotels are surprisingly small, having as few as three rooms. For most forms of accommodation prices are good value compared with Western Europe, even given that foreigners will be charged up to double the price for native Bulgarians.

Bed and breakfast is an excellent budget option throughout the country. Rooms will be simple but spotlessly clean, though they probably won't have private bathrooms. Private room prices per night can be as low as 20 leva, and that includes breakfast. Many of the monasteries offer overnight accommodation to travellers – though it usually won't be in an authentic monk's cell.

There's little pressure on accommodation provision except at times of major festivals, when booking ahead is essential. The Black Sea coast is always full late July–September, when a lot of hotels are commandeered by large tour groups. Out of season (October–May) the majority of the accommodation on the Black Sea closes completely and it may be more difficult to find rooms in private homes across the country.

If you want to travel independently, without making bookings ahead, then you can use the services of the commercial information offices throughout the country. They act as agents for hotels and B&Bs but some are more helpful then others.

The following list of suggested accommodation shows price ranges charged to non-Bulgarians for a double room per night including breakfast. Prices of up-market hotels may be priced in euros or US dollars.

★  budget, under 50 leva
★★  mid range, 50–100 leva
★★★  expensive 100–150 leva
★★★★ very expensive, over 150 leva

## SOFIA

### Radisson SAS ★★★★
Large modern luxury hotel in the heart of the city. Excellent bathrooms and airy rooms make it comfortable. It

incorporates Flannagan's, one of the city's most popular meeting places.
*Pl. Narodno Sabranie 4*
*Tel: (02) 933 43 34*
*Fax: (02) 933 46 00*
*Website*
*www.radissonsas.com*
**Sheraton Sofia Hotel Balkan ★★★★**
A Sofia institution at the heart of the city, this historic hotel has been upgraded in fine style by the Sheraton group.
*Pl. Sveta Nedelya.*
*Tel: (02) 981 65 41.*
*Fax: (02) 980 64 64.*
*www.luxurycollection.com/sofia*
**Hotel Pop Bogomil ★★**
The spacious rooms of this hotel, with their wooden furniture, offer good value for money. Not in the centre – the main square is about a 1km walk – but close to bus and train routes.
*ul. Pop Bogomil 5.*
*Tel: (02) 983 70 65.*
*Fax: (02) 980 43 45.*
**Hotel Sun ★★**
Situated in the lively Lion Bridge quarter, the Sun is housed in an elegant 19th-century building. The café on the ground floor is a busy but atmospheric meeting place. Rooms facing the boulevard may be noisy.

*bul. Maria Louisa 89.*
*Tel: (02) 983 36 70.*
*Fax: (02) 983 53 89.*
**Hotel Lion ★★★★**
New three-star with modern, well-equipped rooms including internet phone connection. Popular with businessmen. Room rates are negotiable at weekends and there's a discount if you pay in cash.
*bul. Maria Louisa 60.*
*Tel/Fax: (02) 917 84 00.*
*www.hotel-lion.net.*
**Hotel Bolide ★**
This tiny hotel is one of the cheapest in the city. Rooms are basic but clean.
*ul. Pop Bogomil 27.*
*Tel: (02) 983 30 02.*
*Fax: (02) 983 59 86.*
**Hotel Central ★★★★**
The Central is one of the first boutique-style hotels in the city, with modern, rather chic décor and facilities such as solarium/sauna and massage centre. There's also a decent restaurant on site.
*bul. Hristo Botev 52.*
*Tel: (02) 981 23 64.*
*Fax: (02) 986 45 61.*

**CENTRAL BULGARIA**
**Tryavna**
**Hotel Zograf ★**
Set in the old town and

opened in 2002, this hotel pays homage to the artisans of Tryavna, being decorated throughout with carved wood. There's a traditional inn on the premises.
*ul. Slaveikov 1.*
*Tel: (0677) 49 70.*
*E-mail:*
*zograf@mbox.digysys.bg*

**Koprivshtitsa**
**Hotel Kalina ★★**
Pretty converted mansion set in a verdant garden next to Karavelov House. The rooms are well equipped and decorated with carved wood detail.
*ul. Hadzhi Nencho Palaveev 35.*
*Tel: (07184) 20 32.*
*E-mail:*
*hotelkalina@fog-bg.net*

**Kazanluk**
**Hotel Hadzhi Eminova Kashta ★**
This is one hotel that charges the same for foreigners at it does for Bulgarians. Built in traditional style in the centre of town, its rooms are simple and bathrooms are on the small side, but there's a good restaurant on site.
*ul. Nikola Petkov 22.*
*Tel: (0431) 420 95.*

## Veliko Turnovo
### Hotel Comfort ★★
Close to the old market in a quiet quarter of the town, the Comfort has newly renovated rooms. There are spectacular views of the light and sound show from some of the rooms.
*Ul. Tipografov 5.*
*Tel: (062) 287 28.*
### Hotel Mehana Gurko ★★★
A small character hotel on one of the cobbled streets of the old town, the Gurko has well-equipped modern rooms (prices are slightly higher than other establishments close by as a consequence), with panoramic views of the town from its balconies. Excellent restaurant on site.
*Ul. Gurko 33.*
*Tel: (062) 78 33.*
*www.hotelgurko.hit.bg*

## Sliven
### Hotel Imperia ★★★★
A place to splash out without breaking the bank, the Imperia is a grand hotel with a swimming pool and sports complex.
*Tel: (044) 850 71.*
*Fax: (044) 807 41.*
*www.hotelimperia.net*

## SOUTHWEST BULGARIA
## Bansko
### Hotel Alpin ★
A converted mansion in the old part of town, the Alpin is a good budget option for this relatively expensive (for Bulgaria) resort. Facilities include a restaurant, sauna and disco in high season.
*Ul. Neofit Rilski 6.*
*Tel: (07443) 80 75.*
*Fax: (07443) 80 77.*
*E-mail: alpin@abv.bg*

## Plovdiv
### Hebros ★★★
In the heart of old Plovdiv, the Hebros is one of a new breed of modern, charming hotels – each room is individually and tastefully decorated, but the price is commensurately high.
*Ul. Stoilov 51.*
*Tel: (032) 260 180.*
*Fax: (032) 260 252.*
*www.hebros-hotel.com*
### Novotel Plovdiv ★★★
This 328-room hotel, part of the French Novotel chain, offers good-quality accommodation with a large pool and two restaurants.
*ul. Zl Bojadgiev 2.*
*Tel: 032 934 444.*
*Fax: 032 934 346.*
*www.novotelpdv.bg*

## Melnik
### Hotel Dospat Slav ★
This restored mansion sits at the end of the town. The rooms are not over-large, but the bathrooms have recently been renovated. There's a good restaurant on site.
*Tel: (07437) 27 1.*
*Fax: (07437) 24 8.*

## Borovets
### Club Alpin ★★
This small hotel at the foot of the pistes has well-equipped rooms and a sauna/jacuzzi for après-ski relaxation. Four-person chalets are also available.
*Tel: (07128) 22 01.*
*Fax: (07128) 22 03.*
*www.alpin-hotel.bg*

## Pamporovo
### Hotel Snezhanska ★★★
A reasonably priced option in what is a very expensive resort by Bulgarian standards, the Snezhanska is open all year. Designed like an alpine chalet, and the rooms are simply furnished. The restaurant serves high-class cuisine.
*Tel: (03021) 83 16.*
*Fax: (03021) 82 73.*
*E-mail:*
*snezhanska@mail.orbitel.bg*

## THE BLACK SEA COAST
### Varna
**Odessos Hotel ★★★**
Large good-quality hotel overlooking Primorski Park in the heart of Varna. A good base for touring the northern Black Sea if you don't want to be in a holiday resort.
*bul. Slivnica 1.*
*Tel: 052 640 300.*
*Fax: 052 630 403.*
*www.odessos-bg.com*
**Vila Sagona ★★**
Set in the verdant landscape of the Primorski Park, the Sagona has tastefully decorated rooms. There's also a swimming pool and one of the best continental restaurants along the Black Sea.
*Primorski Park.*
*Tel: (052) 303 783.*
*Fax: (052) 302 339.*
*www.bgglobe.net/*
*sagona.html*

### Nesebur
**Prince Cyril Hotel ★★**
In the heart of the old town and, unusually for this coast, open all year, the Prince Cyril is set in a rustic traditional Nesebur house, though the rooms are modern and comfortable.
*ul. Slavianska.*
*Tel: (0554) 422 15.*
*E-mail: princecyril@abv.bg*

### Balchik
**Hotel Elit ★**
Just a couple of hundred metres from the entrance to the Palace of Queen Marie, the Elit is a former government residence set in woodland. It makes a good tour stopover, as there is a good-value restaurant on site.
*Road to Varna.*
*Tel: (0579) 769 59.*

### Burgas
**Hotel Boulair ★★**
New hotel (2003) with well-furnished modern rooms but a little lacking in charm. Certainly a good base for touring the southern Black Sea.
*ul. Boulair.*
*Tel: (056) 844 349.*

### Dobrich
**Hotel Bulgaria ★★**
Large central hotel with spacious rooms and facilities such as pool, casino and fitness room. Not bad value at the price, though lacking in character.
*pl. Svoboda.*
*Tel: (058) 601 115.*
*Fax: (058) 601 007.*

## THE NORTH
### Ruse
**Hotel Bistra & Galina ★★**
The group that owns this

hotel operates a society for the development of young Bulgarians. Their training shows in the welcome you get here. The hotel is modern with nicely furnished rooms. Good restaurant on site.
*ul. Asparukh 8.*
*Tel: (082) 33 44.*
*Fax: (082) 33 45.*
*www.bghotel.bg*

### Belogradchik
**Hotel Madona ★**
Family-owned hotel with only three rooms, so it's in demand, the Madona sits by a stream amidst green surroundings. The family also runs a restaurant on site which is the perfect place to spend an evening.
*Ul. Hristo Botev 26.*
*Tel: (0936) 55 46.*
*E-mail:*
*r_mladenov_bg@yahoo.com*

### Vratsa
**Valdi Palace Hotel ★**
This rather dour hotel in the centre of town is like taking a step back to the communist era and it's worth staying here for the nostalgia value. Rooms are comfortable but bland.
*pl. Hristo Botev.*
*Tel: (092) 220 79.*
*Fax: (092) 612 68.*

# Practical Guide

## Arriving
### Entry Formalities

Citizens of all EU countries, Australia, Canada, New Zealand and the USA can enter Bulgaria on a free 30-day tourist visa obtained at the time of arrival at major airports and all border crossings. Citizens of other countries should consult the Bulgarian Embassy in their own country for visa information.

### By Air

The main airport of entry for scheduled flights is Sofia (*Tel: (02) 937 22 12*), though there may be international flights into Varna and Burgas on the Black Sea coast. All major European airlines fly scheduled services into Sofia several times each week:
British Airways (*www.ba.com*),
Air France (*www.airfrance.com*),
KLM (*www.klm.com*) and
Lufthansa (*www.lufthansa.com*).
Balkan Bulgarian Airlines

Sofia is the international air gateway

(*www.balkanair.com*) is the major Bulgarian carrier, offering a network of services to major cities throughout Europe.

There are no direct flights from the USA, Canada, Australia or New Zealand to Bulgaria, though Virgin Atlantic has a code share scheme with Balkan Airlines. Multiple-ticket combinations for flights into Europe and onward to Bulgaria are possible, so it's best to consult a travel agent about the cheapest or most convenient route.

Charter flights are available in winter to Sofia and summer to Varna and Burgas as part of a skiing or Black Sea package tour. Some companies may be happy to offer a flight-only deal but it's also advisable to check prices of flight/hotel packages, as these may offer good value when compared to booking separate flights and hotels.

### Overland

If you are travelling overland (by road or rail) to Bulgaria from the UK or Western Europe, the easiest and quickest route is through the former Yugoslavia. However, because of continued sporadic political turmoil, it is vital to check the advice of the UK Foreign Office or your own government before travelling through this area. Advice below covers travel through the former Yugoslavia and alternatives.

### By Rail

From Italy: daily trains run from Venice through the former Yugoslavia to Sofia on the old Orient Express route.

From Eastern Europe: train services run daily all year from Bucharest to Sofia through Ruse. In summer trains also run to Ruse from Burgas and Varna on the Black Sea coast linking with a service through Bucharest, Budapest and Prague.

From Turkey: daily trains from Istanbul to Bucharest (Romania) have stops in Bulgaria at Stara Zagora, Veliko Turnovo and Ruse.

From Greece: daily trains between Thessalonika and Bucharest have stops in Bulgaria at Blagoevgrad, Sofia, Pleven and Ruse.

Trains often run through the night, so you may find yourself getting off at stations in the small hours of the morning. On some services the booking of a sleeper ticket is compulsory. The *Thomas Cook European Timetable* (*see p186*) contains schedules for all international rail services.

**By Road**
The route through Italy and former Yugoslavia was still not officially considered safe at the time of going to press, but this may change – for the latest information check the British Foreign Office or US State Department website.

There are land crossings into Bulgaria through Romania, Greece and Turkey. Travelling through Greece is the easiest and shortest option from the UK, with a well-organised and comfortable Italy–Greece ferry service (try Superfast Ferries; *www.superfast.com*) allowing you to reach Bulgaria from the UK in 4 days. Sail from Ancona, Venice or Bari in Italy to Iguoumenitsa or Patras on the west coast of Greece for onward road

travel to the land border at Kulata, south of Sofia in Bulgaria.

Make sure you have insurance cover for the vehicle – this may involve getting a Green Card extension to your normal insurance policy.

**Arriving by Coach**
Eurolines (*www.eurolines.co.uk*) runs several services per week from locations in the UK to Bulgaria, though this may involve transfers. The journey takes at least three days.

**Camping**
Facilities for campers are poor compared with Western European countries. Many have had little investment since the communist era. The best sites are on the Black Sea coast, though these get crowded in July and August, when it's best to book in advance, and they close in winter (October–May).

**Children**
Stocks of essentials such as nappies and baby food can be found in towns all across Bulgaria but you may have problems finding child-friendly changing places. High seats in restaurants are non-existent outside the major package-tour hotels.

If you travel with children during the summer make sure you adequately protect them against the strong sun. Mosquitoes may be a problem so take insect repellent and after walking through the countryside check for midge or tick bites. Don't allow children to play with animals, as rabies, though not common, is a danger.

## Climate

Bulgarian weather is characterised by hot dry summers and cool-to-cold, damp winters.

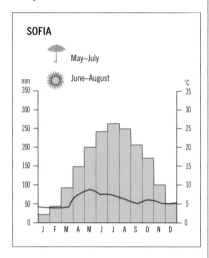

SOFIA

May–July

June–August

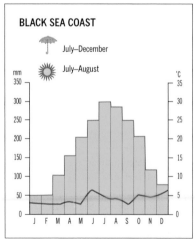

BLACK SEA COAST

July–December

July–August

**Weather Conversion Chart**
25.4mm = 1 inch
°F = 1.8 x °C + 32

Summer temperatures are tempered in the east by the Black Sea. The mountains receive more rain and snow than the plains but winter can produce massive rain and snowfall across the whole country.

## Conversion Tables

Bulgaria uses the European continental clothing size system (*see table*).

## Crime

You'll be at a relatively low risk of becoming a victim of serious crime in Bulgaria. However, so-called petty crime such as theft (especially from vehicles) can be a problem in big cities or on the Black Sea coast. Take the following precautions to minimise your chances of a loss.

Do not leave valuables in a car and leave nothing on show.

Don't carry large amounts of cash or valuables with you.

Deposit valuables in the hotel safe.

Take extra care at cashpoint machines.

Carry handbags over your shoulder and across your chest to thwart bag snatchers.

Don't leave valuables unattended on the beach or in cafés and restaurants.

## Customs Regulations

Foreigners over 16 are allowed to take in the following items duty-free:

200 cigarettes or 250g of tobacco
2l of wine or 1l of stronger alcohol
500g of coffee
50ml of perfume

Bulgarian currency up to the amount of 50,000 leva may be imported or exported without restriction.

## Driving

Although driving is by far the best way of seeing the wonderful countryside, it presents several challenges. Bulgaria drives on the right, overtaking on the left. Roads vary greatly in quality. The main link roads are acceptable but may have areas where the upper layer of tarmac has been removed. Minor roads are in poor condition and riddled with potholes.

Traffic is a combination of modern juggernaut trucks, modern family cars, slow farm vehicles and horse-drawn carriages. Road signs are in Cyrillic only (except in Sofia and on the Black Sea coast) and some are missing, making navigating a challenge.

Speed limits for cars are 120kp/h on dual carriageways, 90kp/h on main roads and 50kp/h in urban areas. Seat belts are compulsory for driver and front seat passenger and helmets compulsory for motorcyclists. The blood-alcohol limit is 0.05% and it is strictly enforced. It's compulsory to wait with the vehicle until the police arrive if you have an accident.

### Car Rental

Cars can be rented in Sofia and in the major resorts and towns. The international car rental companies may charge up to 50 per cent more than a local agency; you will, however, get a new car and good back-up if you have a problem. Renting through a local agency will be cheaper but cars may be older and not all companies accept credit cards, which means leaving cash as a deposit (normally around €150). Many Bulgarian travel agencies/commercial tourist offices will also organise car rental.

### Conversion Table

| FROM | TO | MULTIPLY BY |
|------|-----|-------------|
| Inches | Centimetres | 2.54 |
| Feet | Metres | 0.3048 |
| Yards | Metres | 0.9144 |
| Miles | Kilometres | 1.6090 |
| Acres | Hectares | 0.4047 |
| Gallons | Litres | 4.5460 |
| Ounces | Grams | 28.35 |
| Pounds | Grams | 453.6 |
| Pounds | Kilograms | 0.4536 |
| Tons | Tonnes | 1.0160 |

To convert back, for example from centimetres to inches, divide by the number in the third column.

### Men's Suits

| | | | | | | | |
|---|---|---|---|---|---|---|---|
| UK | 36 | 38 | 40 | 42 | 44 | 46 | 48 |
| Bulgaria & Rest of Europe | 46 | 48 | 50 | 52 | 54 | 56 | 58 |
| USA | 36 | 38 | 40 | 42 | 44 | 46 | 48 |

### Dress Sizes

| | | | | | | |
|---|---|---|---|---|---|---|
| UK | 8 | 10 | 12 | 14 | 16 | 18 |
| France | 36 | 38 | 40 | 42 | 44 | 46 |
| Italy | 38 | 40 | 42 | 44 | 46 | 48 |
| Bulgaria & Rest of Europe | 34 | 36 | 38 | 40 | 42 | 44 |
| USA | 6 | 8 | 10 | 12 | 14 | 16 |

### Men's Shirts

| | | | | | | | |
|---|---|---|---|---|---|---|---|
| UK | 14 | 14.5 | 15 | 15.5 | 16 | 16.5 | 17 |
| Bulgaria & Rest of Europe | 36 | 37 | 38 | 39/40 | 41 | 42 | 43 |
| USA | 14 | 14.5 | 15 | 15.5 | 16 | 16.5 | 17 |

### Men's Shoes

| | | | | | | | |
|---|---|---|---|---|---|---|---|
| UK | 7 | 7.5 | 8.5 | | 9.5 | 10.5 | 11 |
| Bulgaria & Rest of Europe | 41 | 42 | 43 | | 44 | 45 | 46 |
| USA | 8 | 8.5 | 9.5 | | 10.5 | 11.5 | 12 |

### Women's Shoes

| | | | | | | |
|---|---|---|---|---|---|---|
| UK | 4.5 | 5 | 5.5 | 6 | 6.5 | 7 |
| Bulgaria & Rest of Europe | 38 | 38 | 39 | 39 | 40 | 41 |
| USA | 6 | 6.5 | 7 | 7.5 | 8 | 8.5 |

## Driving Licences

Your domestic driving licence is recognised in Bulgaria as long as you stay less than 3 months. You will need to have had a full licence for at least one year and be over 21 to rent a vehicle.

## Electricity

Bulgaria uses 220v AC for its supply. Plugs are the two-pinned variety, so travellers from the UK will need an adapter.

## Embassies and Consulates

All foreign embassies and consulates are located in the capital, Sofia.

**UK**
*ul. Moskovska 9. Tel: (02) 933 9222; Fax: (02) 933 9219.*

**USA**
*ul. Saborna 1. Tel: (02) 953 5100; Fax: (02) 981 9358.*

**Australian Consulate**
*ul. Trakia 37. Tel: (02) 946 1331; Fax: (02) 946 1704.*

**Canadian Consulate**
*ul. Assen Zlatarov 11. Tel: (02) 943 3704; Fax: (02) 946 1913.*

**Republic of Ireland**
*bul. Stamboliiski 55. Tel: (02) 981 2094. Fax: (02) 981 5389.*

**Emergency Telephone Numbers**
**Fire** *160*
**Ambulance** *150*
**Police** *166*
**Traffic Police** *165*

## Health

There are no compulsory inoculations for travel to Bulgaria.

There is basic health care (a clinic) in most small towns and there are hospitals in major towns, but these are under-equipped by Western European standards. Sofia has the best-equipped and also has several private hospitals. Doctors are well trained and most speak some English. UK citizens can receive treatment without charge but citizens of other countries must pay at time of treatment in local currency (take receipts to claim money back from your insurance company). *See also Insurance p181.*

Pharmacies sell many drugs over the counter; however, brand names vary, so if you need a specific medication/drug take an empty packet with you to aid the pharmacist.

Several minor nuisances should be watched for. Mosquitoes can be a problem so carry repellent and cover arms and legs in the evenings. It is wise to cover legs and arms when hiking in undergrowth. Ticks can carry encephalitis (from May to September), so after hiking check that you haven't been bitten; if you have and you experience flu-like symptoms, seek immediate medical advice, as the condition needs early treatment.

Road sign: only major towns are signposted in Roman script

## Insurance

Having adequate insurance cover is vital. UK citizens will be treated without charge at public hospitals in Bulgaria but a travel insurance policy will allow service at a private hospital and repatriation if the injuries/illness warrants it. All other nationalities should ensure adequate cover for illness or accident as they will be charged at point of treatment.

Travellers should always have cover for everything they carry with them in case of loss or theft. Insurance companies also usually provide cover for cancellation or travel delay in their policies. Though not essential cover this offers some compensation if travel plans go awry.

## Lost Property

Airports and railway stations have lost property departments, otherwise try the local police station. You'll need an official police report to make an insurance claim for any lost property. If you lose your passport contact your Embassy or Consulate immediately.

## Maps

You can buy maps of Bulgaria at all major bookstores, but these may be in Cyrillic only. Domino (*www.domino.bg*) produces the best range.

## Media

The *Sofia Echo* (*www.sofiaecho.com*) is an English-language newspaper published each Friday. It has details of entertainment listings as well as news. Foreign newspapers are available in Sofia and the Black Sea resorts, though these may be one day old. Internet cafés are common and access is cheap.

Multilingual signs are common in the Black Sea resorts

# LANGUAGE

Bulgarian is a Slavic language written in Cyrillic script, an alphabet with 30 letters. Though most workers in the tourist industry speak some English, it will certainly help your visit if you have a basic understanding of this alphabet.

## THE CYRILLIC ALPHABET

All letters are pronounced as their Roman equivalents in English unless indicated otherwise.

| Capital | Lower-case | Roman | Pronunciation |
|---|---|---|---|
| А | а | a | short as in 'fat' |
| Б | б | b | |
| В | в | v | |
| Г | г | gh | hard as in 'go' |
| Д | д | d | |
| Е | е | e | |
| Ж | ж | zh | as the s in 'treasure' |
| З | з | z | |
| И | и | i | |
| Й | й | y | |
| К | к | k | |
| Л | л | l | |
| М | m | m | |
| Н | н | n | |
| О | о | o | short as in 'hot' |
| П | П | p | |
| Р | р | r | a rolling r like that of French |
| С | с | s | |
| Т | т | t | |
| У | у | u | as in 'shut' |
| Ф | ф | f | |
| Х | х | ch | like the ch of Scottish 'loch' |
| Ц | ц | ts | as in the word 'bets' |
| Ч | ч | ch | as in 'chop' |
| Ш | ш | sh | as in 'shop' |
| Щ | щ | sht | as the 'shed' in 'rushed' but shorter |
| Ъ | ъ | u | Short u sound like German 'ö' or French 'eu'. |
| Ь | ь | û | as in the French 'tu' |
| Я | я | ya | a short hard sound |
| Ю | ю | yu | a short hard sound |

**PHRASES**

Here are a few helpful phrases written in Cyrillic script, then in Roman script so that you can understand how to pronounce them.

| English | Cyrillic | Roman |
|---------|----------|-------|
| Hello | Здравейте | zdraveyte |
| Goodbye | Довиждане | dovizhdane |
| Yes | Да | da |
| No | Не | ne |
| Please | Моля | molya |
| Thank you | Благодаря | blagodarya |
| Do you speak English | Говорите ли английски | govorite li angliyski |
| I don't understand | Аз Не разбирам | az ne razbiram |
| I am looking for the/a | Търся | târysa |
| Bank | Банка | banka |
| Museum | Музея | muzeya |
| Post office | Поща | poshta |
| Toilet | Тоалетна | toaletna |
| Tourist office | Бюрото за туризъм | byuroto za turizâm |
| Hotel | Хотел | khotel |
| How much is it? | Колко струва? | kolko struva? |
| Monday | Понеделник | Ponedelnik |
| Tuesday | Вторник | Vtornik |
| Wednesday | Сряда | Sryada |
| Thursday | Четвъртък | Chetvârtâk |
| Friday | Петък | Petâk |
| Saturday | Събота | Sâbota |
| Sunday | Неделя | Nedelya |
| One | едно | edno |
| Two | две | dve |
| Three | три | tri |
| Four | четири | chetiri |
| Five | пет | pet |
| Six | шест | shest |
| Seven | седем | sedem |
| Eight | осем | osem |
| Nine | девет | devet |
| Ten | десет | deset |
| One hundred | сто | sto |
| Help! | помош | Pomosh! |

ПОЩЕНСКИ КОД **5000**

•ПОЩА• POSTE•

ПИСМАТА СЕ СЪБИРАТ
В 14 часа

Post boxes are yellow

## Money Matters
### Currency

Bulgarian currency is the lev, leva in the plural, abbreviated lv in shops, hotels and restaurants, or BGN in banks and bureaux de change. One lev is made up of 100 stotinki, with note denominations of 1, 2, 5, 10, 20 and 50 leva and coins of 1, 2, 5, 10, 20 and 50 stotinki. Since the introduction of the euro, the lev has been linked to it at an exchange rate of 1.96lv to 1 euro. All other currencies fluctuate with the exchange markets. If bringing foreign banknotes to exchange in Bulgaria ensure that none are defaced or torn as they may be refused.

### Foreign Exchange

Although prices for restaurants and budget hotels will be quoted in leva, most expensive purchases (higher grade hotels, car hire, excursions etc) will be quoted in euros or US dollars. It will be possible to pay for these items in most forms of foreign currency at the day's exchange rate. Foreign currency can be exchanged at bureaux de change, which are plentiful at resorts and in major towns. Most large banks will also offer an exchange rate facility. Travellers will find it easier if they carry US dollars, euros or pounds sterling rather than any other foreign currency, which may be less easy to change.

Traveller's cheques are not as easy to cash as foreign currency (though they are more secure than cash, as you can get them replaced if they are lost or stolen).

ATMs are becoming more numerous and you will certainly be able to get cash in Sofia and the Black Sea coast resorts. Before you travel check that your bank has an agreement with the banking system in Bulgaria.

### Credit cards

Credit cards are not universally accepted across Bulgaria but their use is gaining ground. If you intend to stay in the capital or on the Black Sea you'll find their use more widespread (though you may be subject to a surcharge) but it's still better to ask at hotels, restaurants and petrol stations before you order if you intend to pay with a card (some have window stickers but no card facilities!). It is also wise to carry enough cash to cover your daily needs just in case. You can use your credit card to get cash advances over the counter in some banks.

### Opening Hours

Normal business hours are Mon–Fri 9am–5pm. Government offices will close for an hour at lunchtime (anytime between noon and 2pm) but commercial organisations generally don't. Shops open Mon–Fri 9am–7pm and Sat 9am–1pm, but have extended hours in summer, especially in Sofia and on the Black Sea coast. Post offices are open Mon–Fri 8am–6pm. Banks are open Mon–Fri 9am–4pm. Museums are generally open 10am–5.30pm but are closed at least one day and many close at lunchtimes for one hour. Opening times change frequently.

## Police

Police officers wear navy blue uniforms, rather like overalls. They aren't universally helpful and many don't speak English, but they are not a problem for ordinary law-abiding visitors. There are also numerous armed private security guards in shops and banks; they have no jurisdiction under law but have been employed to thwart shoplifters and crime gangs. If this makes Bulgaria sound like a dangerous or lawless place don't worry, because it isn't.
*Emergency
Tel: 166.*

## Post Offices

Post office signs are yellow with a black bugle imprinted on them. You'll find post offices in all major towns and many

post boxes, also yellow. Postcard shops in the resorts will sell stamps.

## Public Holidays

The following dates are official holidays in Bulgaria. All government buildings and banks will be closed but not commercial businesses. Public transport also operates normally.

**1st Jan** New Year's Day
**3rd Mar** Liberation or National Day
**Mar/April** Good Friday and Easter Sunday
**6th May** St George's Day
**24th May** Bulgarian Culture Day
**6th Sept** National Day or Unification Day
**22 Sept** Bulgarian Independence Day
**1 Nov** National Revival Day
**25th–26th Dec** Christmas

## Public Transport
### Air

Internal flights are limited to travel between Sofia and Varna airport on the Black Sea coast. Balkan Airlines runs 2–4 flights a day, depending on the season, all year. There are other airlines running summer flights (normally Apr–Oct), with prices much the same as the main carrier.

Bulgarian traffic cop

**Trains**

Bulgarski Durzhavni Zheleznitsi (ЧДЖ), the Bulgarian state railway, has a comprehensive network linking all the major settlements. It is cheap, but the rolling stock and track is not up to Western standards. Trains are classified as *ekspresen* (express), *burz* (fast), and *putnicheski* (slow). First-class fares are only around 20% higher than second class. Bookable sleeper couchettes are available on longer journeys. Advance tickets are recommended if you want to travel to the Black Sea from Sofia. Most European rail passes are valid in Bulgaria and the Bulgarian system is also linked to the Euro-Domino pass. Timetables are available but are only in Cyrillic. For a timetable of the main Bulgarian rail services, consult the *Thomas Cook European Timetable*, published monthly and available from UK branches of Thomas Cook or through *tel: 01733 (+44 1733) 416477, www.thomascookpublishing.com.*

**Buses**

A network of public buses run by the government connects almost all towns and villages in the country. Fares are cheap but many buses are antiquated and you can't book ahead. In larger towns and cities modern private bus services now offer a much more acceptable alternative and a reliable way to get around, with the added advantage that you can book tickets in advance from the ticket office at the bus station.

Minibuses link the resorts along the Black Sea coast. You can normally buy tickets from the driver.

Local bus

Taxi, Sofia

## Taxis

Taxis are painted yellow and are numerous in cities and resorts. They can be flagged down in the street. They must by law have a working meter but can be chartered for longer trips – negotiate with the driver. Taxi drivers along the Black Sea coast and around the railway station and airport in Sofia have a reputation for overcharging, so don't agree to a flat rate or believe stories of meters not working.

### Telephones

The public telephone system is undergoing rapid development with booths in major cities and towns offering international direct dialling by credit card (where the instructions will be shown in English) or local phone card. For local calls buy tokens, available at newspaper stands and general stores.

Bulgarian Telecommunications Company (BTC) is the national provider and it has a network of call centres in all

major towns. Here you can make calls, including long-distance and international calls, and pay for them on completion.

Modern hotels will usually have a direct dial phone system, but they often add extortionate surcharges for calls. Ask about charges before you make the decision to ring home.

The country code for phoning from abroad to Bulgaria is 359; then omit the first 0 in the Bulgarian area code that follows. To make an international call from inside Bulgaria dial 00 followed by the country code, for example:

**USA and Canada** 00 1
**UK** 00 44
**Ireland** 00 353
**Australia** 00 61
**New Zealand** 00 64

Telephone booth

## Time

Bulgaria is on Eastern European time, GMT + 2 hours. Since it has no added hour in summer time, this puts it 2 hours ahead of the UK during the winter, but only 1 hour ahead during British Summer Time (end Mar–end Oct). From Nov to end May, when it is noon in Sofia it is 10am in London, 8pm in Sydney and 5am in New York and Toronto.

## Tipping

Some hotels and restaurants add a service charge to the bill. If not, a 10% tip is usual if the service has been good. Don't put tips in the hand, as this is socially unacceptable. Taxi drivers may round the fare up, in which case they don't need a tip.

A commercial tourist office

## Toilets

Most toilets are the sit-on variety, though you may find some 'hole in the floor' type in the southeast. Public toilets are generally poor in quality and cleanliness, even though there is usually a charge to use them. Better to try to use facilities in museums (generally good) or bar/restaurants (of mixed quality). Always carry a supply of toilet paper with you.

## Tourist Information

Bulgaria is still a long way from providing a comprehensive and integrated tourist information service. Most 'tourist offices' in towns are commercial organisations geared to booking accommodation and bus tours.

Before you travel you can obtain general brochures from your local Bulgarian National Tourist Office or Embassy at one of these addresses:
**Australia** *4 Carlotta Road, Double Bay, NSW 2028. Tel: 02 9362 9838.*
**Canada** *325 Stewart Street, Ottawa, Ontario K1N 6K5. Tel: 0613 789 5341.*
**UK** *186–188 Queen's Gate, London SW7 5HL. Tel: 020 7589 8402.*
**USA** *1621 22nd St NW, Washington DC 20008. Tel: 0202 332 6609.*

## Travellers with Disabilities

Provision for travellers with mobility problems is poor. Always make specific enquiries with hotels if you require specially equipped rooms.
In the UK, Holiday Care Services *(Tel: 0845 124 9971; www.holidaycare.org.uk)* has holiday and travel information for people with disabilities.

# Sustainable Travel

**Caring for Places we Visit**

The Travel Foundation is a UK charity that cares for places we love to visit. You can help us protect the natural environment, traditions and culture – the things that make your visit special. And improve the well-being of local families – spreading the benefit of your visit to those who most need it. All of which can make your holiday experience even better! Most importantly, you can help ensure that there are great places for us all to visit – for generations to come.

What you can do:

- Remove any packaging from items before you go on holiday and recycle if possible.
- Do hire local guides and book locally-run excursions – it will enrich your holiday experience and help support local families.
- Hire a car only if you need to. Using public transport, bicycles and walking are environmentally-friendlier alternatives.
- Respect local culture and traditions. Ensure your dress and behaviour is appropriate for the places you visit. Ask permission before taking photographs of people or their homes.
- Turn down/off heating or air conditioning when not required. Switch off lights and turn the television off rather than leave on standby.

- Do use water sparingly. Take showers instead of baths and inform staff if you are happy to re-use towels and bed linen rather than replace daily.
- Don't pick flowers and plants or collect pebbles, seashells, coral or starfish. Leave them for others to enjoy.
- Don't buy products made from endangered plants or animals, including hardwoods, ivory, corals, reptiles or turtles. If in doubt – don't buy.
- Do buy locally-made products – shopping in locally-owned outlets and treating yourself to local food and drink is a great way to get into the holiday spirit and also benefits local families.
- Always bargain with humour and bear in mind that a small cash saving to you could be a significant amount to the seller.
- Coral is extremely fragile. Don't step on it or remove it, and avoid kicking up sand.

For more tips and information on The Travel Foundation and its work, please visit
*www.thetravelfoundation.org.uk*

the
**travel foundation**
caring for places we love to visit

**ACKNOWLEDGEMENTS**

Thomas Cook Publishing wishes to thank Pete Bennett for the photographs in this book.

**FOR LABURNUM TECHNOLOGIES**

| | | | |
|---|---|---|---|
| **Design Director** | Alpana Khare | **Designer** | Neeraj Aggarwal |
| **Series Director** | Razia Grover | **DTP Designer** | Harish Aggarwal |
| **Editors** | Madhumadhavi Singh, Sunanda Lahiri | **Photo Editor** | Manju Singhal |

Thanks to Stephen York for the Index.